Pascal
from
BASIC

P. J. BROWN
University of Kent at Canterbury

ADDISON-WESLEY PUBLISHING COMPANY
in association with
ACORNSФFT

Wokingham, Berkshire · Reading, Massachusetts
Menlo Park, California · Amsterdam · Don Mills, Ontario
Manila · Singapore · Sydney · Tokyo

© 1982 by Addison-Wesley Publishers Limited
This edition published 1984 by Addison-Wesley Publishers Limited,
Finchampstead Road, Wokingham, Berkshire, in association with Acornsoft.

Composition in Times by Filmtype Services Limited,
Scarborough, North Yorkshire.

Printed in Finland by Werner Söderström Osakeyhtiö, Member of Finnprint

British Library Cataloguing in Publication Data
Brown, P. J.
 Pascal from BASIC.
 1. PASCAL (Computer program language)
 I. Title
 001.64'24   QA76.73P2

 ISBN 0–201–13789–5

Contents

To my wife who nagged me to finish;
     my girlfriend who kept me cheerful;
     my colleague who criticized;
     my boss who understands me all too well.

To the one person who is all of these.

The publishers wish to thank Dave Farris for the cartoon illustrations.

Preface

VISITOR: *Can you tell me the way to the Post Office?*

LOCAL: *If I was going to the Post Office I wouldn't start from here.*

This book assumes that you are a reasonably competent BASIC programmer and that you want to learn Pascal. Most Pascal books are written as if the reader does not know how to program. Your problem is quite different, however, from that of the novice. You do not want explanations of basic concepts such as variables, loops and so on, but you do want help in adjusting your manner of thinking from BASIC to Pascal. In fact your task is probably *harder* than that of the novice, because BASIC is actually a maverick among programming languages – though it has become the world's most popular language in spite of (because of?) this. It is harder to learn concepts and then to relearn them in a new way, than to start from scratch. Make no mistake, switching from BASIC to Pascal does mean a radical change. If you write your Pascal programs in the same way as your BASIC programs you will be like an English-speaking tourist in France translating your sentences word for word from a dictionary.

This book is aimed specifically to help you conquer the problems that BASIC programmers have with Pascal, and to adapt your programming style accordingly. It is not assumed that you are forsaking your old friend BASIC entirely. Instead the book is quite critical of some aspects of Pascal, and tries to make clear to you where Pascal gains and where it loses.

The book also aims to be light, and fun to read. The goal is to be serious without being solemn and stodgy. Concepts are introduced almost entirely in terms of examples, and, where relevant, these are related to BASIC. If you prefer a more formal approach, look elsewhere.

When you read this book you should gain two capabilities. You should be able to write good Pascal programs, and to read Pascal reference manuals and appreciate what they are all about.

The book is strenuously neutral towards competing versions of Pascal: with absolute fairness, it does not mention any of them. Fortunately, different Pascal systems are much more similar than are BASIC systems, so it is possible to give a detailed discussion without commitment to a particular implementation. Thus it is immaterial whether you are planning to use Pascal on a personal computer or on a large time-shared mainframe computer.

Acknowledgements

I would like to thank Laurence Atkinson who, by his enthusiasm, unknowingly inspired me to write this book. Thanks are also due to Tony Hoare for valuable guidance and to several of my colleagues, including Stephen Binns, David Turner and, most especially, Peter Welch. A kind and friendly Pascal system provided the layout of the programs shown in this book.

Finally let me record my gratitude to two of the world's greatest. Marianne Kong typed the manuscript with amazing care and conscientiousness, and put up nobly with all my changes. Heather Brown spent as many hours in checking and criticizing as I did in writing. Her caustic comments and her savage condemnations annihilated the worst parts of the book before they reached print.

Canterbury   Peter Brown
October 1981

CHAPTER 1

An example to show the fundamentals

begin *at the beginning.*

DYLAN THOMAS

An example

To get a feel for the task in hand, we shall start with a very simple BASIC program and show its Pascal equivalent. The program takes as data a number N, which is followed by N further numbers. All the program does is to print the average of the numbers. In BASIC the program can be written

```
10   REM---FINDS THE AVERAGE OF N NUMBERS---
100 INPUT N
110 LET S = 0
120 FOR K = 1 TO N
130    INPUT X
140     LET S = S + X
150 NEXT K
200 PRINT"AVERAGE =";S/N
999 END
```

A direct translation of this into Pascal – which, as we shall see, is not a good Pascal program – is

```
program average(input, output);

{ ---finds the average of N numbers--- }

var
    n: integer;
    k: integer;
    s: real;
    x: real;

begin
    read(n);
    s := 0;
    for k := 1 to n do
    begin
        read (x);
        s := s + x;
    end;
    writeln ('Average =', s/n);
end.
```

If you have never seen a Pascal program before, many differences from BASIC will strike you straight away.

The most manifest is, paradoxically, one of the least significant: the fact that the BASIC program uses upper case letters (i.e. capital letters) whereas the Pascal program uses lower case. The first point to make is that this is largely a matter of habit rather than requirement. We could have written the BASIC program in lower case and the Pascal in upper case, and the programs would still be acceptable to most compilers.

The habit – and it is not a universal habit – of using upper case letters in BASIC results largely from history. BASIC grew up in the early sixties when computers had very small character sets; input to computers was often from punched cards or primitive typewriters, and lower case letters were usually not available. More recently, computers and devices for entering data into computers have supported richer character sets. You no longer have to SHOUT AT THE COMPUTER IN UPPER CASE, but can communicate in a much more refined way in lower case. The pendulum has now swung so far that many programmers avoid upper case altogether, and programming manuals for more recent languages tend to do likewise. Doubtless it will swing back one day to a more moderate position.

The current convention is, however, quite useful for this book. We shall present BASIC programs in upper case and Pascal programs in lower case. We can thus talk about and compare programs without ambiguity.

It can also be seen that the Pascal program contains bold face words, such as **begin**. Again, this is a habit of presentation rather than a fundamental property of the language. When you type the program into the computer you type the bold face letters as ordinary letters.

Declarations

A second striking facet of the programs is that in BASIC the action starts in line one (or, strictly speaking, line two as the first line is a comment), whereas in the Pascal program there are half a dozen lines of introduction before anything actually happens. The first line is

program *average*(*input*, *output*);

A line of this form needs to come at the start of every Pascal program – the name you choose to give the program, in this case *average*, being inserted into what is almost a fixed template. We shall explain this program heading line later. The line after the program heading is a Pascal comment, akin to a REM in BASIC.

Much more important are the lines

var
    n: *integer*;
    k: *integer*;
    s: *real*;
    x: *real*;

These are examples of *declaration*s. In BASIC, if you want to use a variable X you can do so with no fuss or preparation; in Pascal, on the other hand, you must declare the variable X before you can use it. BASIC does, of course, contain the concept of declarations. If you want to use an array (table) Q in BASIC you need to declare it by a line such as

DIM Q (5, 8)

Pascal has the same idea, but you have to declare *everything*.

When you declare a variable you need to specify its *data type*. Data types are one of the most powerful and exciting features of Pascal, though this is not brought out by our present sample program. Pascal has some built-in data types, like the *integer* and *real* types used above, and also allows you to define your own types, as we shall see. BASIC has an embryo idea of data type. Variables are normally of *numeric* data type, as N, K, S and X in our example. However, if a dollar sign is appended to its name a variable is of *string* data type, e.g. A$, P9$. Some BASICs also support an *integer* data type, often represented by names such as K%, T%.

A data type specifies the set of values that an object may take. Associated with each data type is a set of operators; you can for example apply a multiplication operator to numeric data. You cannot multiply two strings together, but there are other operations that apply uniquely to strings, such as extracting a substring. Some operators are *polymorphic* in that they apply to more than one data type. In BASIC this applies, for example, to the assignment operator, and to some operators on IF statements, e.g.

```
LET X = 3
LET X$ = "STRING"

IF X = Y THEN 30
IF X$ = Y$ THEN 50
```

Similar rules apply to Pascal. BASIC data types are manifest from the name of a variable: X is numeric and X$ is a string. In Pascal any name can be used for any variable. When you declare the variable you give its name and its associated data type. We shall see later that there is freedom of choice with Pascal names. We could, and indeed should, have used the name *sum* or even the name *sumofvariables* rather than the name *s*. As a general principle it is better to choose names that make the purpose of the variables clear; our use of single character names was to maintain a direct correspondence with BASIC.

The data types used in the *average* program are *real*, which is the same as the numeric type of BASIC, and *integer*. The variables *s* and *x* are declared to be real variables, and *n* and *k* to be integer variables. (We could have written these four declarations in any order, just as in BASIC you can declare arrays in any order.) It is important in Pascal to distinguish variables that can only take on integer values, like *n* and *k* in the *average* program, from those that can take any numeric value, like *s* and *x*. The reasons for this stem mainly from the design of current computers. If a variable is known to take only integer values, it can be stored in a different and more compact way from a variable that can take any numeric value. Moreover, operations on integers run much faster than on real values; the factor may range from two to over one hundred. Finally, the integer operations are exact. Real operations are inexact, and can give small round-off errors. You may well have experienced the effects of this round-off when running a BASIC program; perhaps you expected the answer 6 from a program and instead the answer came back as 6.000000001.

In most BASICs you ignore the difference between integers and real numbers by making everything real (numeric), and you put up with the occasional eccentricity such as the 6.000000001. In Pascal you can sometimes get away with this, but cannot use a real variable on a **for** statement or as an array subscript. Given these requirements and their indirect consequences, it is best to distinguish integers from reals. The only possible problem with using the integer data type is that some implementations place quite severe limits on the size of integers – integers may, for example, be forbidden from exceeding 32,767. Consult your local manual for details.

The program

When you look at the executable instructions in the Pascal program you are on more familiar ground. The statements in the Pascal example are in one-to-one correspondence with the BASIC example except that Pascal has a couple of **begin**s and **end**s. The **begin**s and **end**s are one of the *structuring* concepts of Pascal. Favourite concepts in programming come and go, but structuring has remained on the best sellers' list for several years now. The reason is quite fundamental: the only way we can hope to understand a large program is to build it out of smaller and simpler substructures.

To get an idea of the purpose of **begin** and **end** it is instructive to consider two examples of FOR statements in BASIC and Pascal

BASIC	*Pascal*
10 FOR K = 1 TO 10	**for** $k := 1$ **to** 10 **do**
20 LET S = S + K	$s := s + k;$
30 NEXT K	
60 FOR K = 1 TO 10	**for** $k := 1$ **to** 10 **do**
70 LET S = S + K	**begin**
80 LET T = T + K * K	$s := s + k;$
90 NEXT K	$t := t + k * k;$
	end;

The FOR statement is the only structuring construct in standard minimal BASIC. Each FOR is matched by a NEXT and the statements in between are treated as a unit. In Pascal there are many structuring constructs within programs, of which **for** is one. Several of these constructs use **begin** and **end** to enclose a group of statements that is to be treated as a single unit. This unit is called a *compound statement*. The **for** construction in Pascal is not in itself a statement. It is a *clause* that must be prefixed to a single statement. If you want to make several statements the subject of the **for** you put a **begin** and **end** round them; this turns them into a compound statement, which counts as a single statement. In our first **for** example above we do not need a **begin** and **end** because there is only one statement to be iterated. However it does not matter if you insert extra redundant **begin**s and **end**s, so we could have put them in. Our second example needs the **begin** and **end** because more than one statement is to be repeated.

The body of an entire Pascal program is enclosed by a **begin** and **end**. The final **end** is written

   end.

The dot means it is the very end of the program. Like FOR and NEXT, **begin** and **end** nest in a natural way, e.g.

```
begin {A}
    {...}
begin {B}
    {...}
end; {B}
    {...}
begin {C}
    {...}
end; {C}
    {...}
end; {A}
```

Here, the **begin** we have marked with the comment {A} matches the **end** similarly marked, and so on. A good program is laid out so that it is visually obvious which **begins** and **ends** match e.g.

```
begin
    {...}
    begin
        {...}
    end;
    {...}
    begin
        {...}
    end;
    {...}
end;
```

It is, of course, wrong to have **begins** that are not matched by **ends** or vice-versa.

You will find that, because of the preponderance of structuring concepts in Pascal, a little care in program layout will reap big rewards in readability. If you are lucky, you will have a 'prettyprinting' utility on your computer. This is a program that takes a Pascal program and turns it into a decently laid out form. (Prettyprinters also exist for BASIC, but the task is a smaller one.) However, although such programs are useful for a final tidy up, it is much better for you to get in the habit of laying out programs decently from the outset.

Individual statements

The individual statements in our *average* program are similar in both BASIC and Pascal, e.g.

BASIC	*Pascal*
INPUT N	*read(n);*
LET S = S + X	*s := s + x;*
PRINT "AVERAGE="; S/N	*writeln('Average =', s / n);*

Pascal, unfortunately from the point of view of the BASIC programmer, uses *read* to mean INPUT. Pascal has no concept similar to READ in BASIC, so if you mistakenly use *read* to try to READ you will soon find that you are attempting the impossible.

The Pascal assignment statement has no LET, but many BASICs allow LET to be omitted. More trying is the ': =' that must be typed in Pascal for BASIC's '='. (This applies to **for** statements as well, as a glance back to previous examples will show.)

The simple output statements in BASIC and Pascal are fundamentally similar. The name *writeln* is a somewhat unfortunate shortening of what might have been called *writeline*, but was not.

Finally you have doubtless observed that each Pascal statement has a semicolon on the end. In BASIC, statements are related to lines of the program. In Pascal the end of a line is treated just like a space, so an explicit marker is needed at the end of a statement. If you had a terminal with a fantastically wide line, you could type an entire Pascal program on a single line.

As a more prosaic example, the Pascal lines

$x := $
$3 ;$
$y := 4;$

and

$x := 3; y := 4;$

are identical in meaning.

Normally, however, it is best not to take advantage of the flexibility offered. Until you get used to Pascal and develop a style of layout of your own, it is wise to put one statement on each line.

Strictly speaking a semicolon *separates* rather than terminates statements. This means you do not need a semicolon after the last statement in a group, i.e. after the statement preceding an **end**. If you do put a semicolon before **end**, as we have done in all examples so far, you have in fact written a *null statement* before the **end**. Null statements cause no action and do no harm. If your finger gets stuck to the semicolon key and you type

$x := 3;;;;$

you will have typed three null statements, but your program will not be affected. Pascal, like most of us, does not mind doing nothing.

We shall stick with our convention of putting a semicolon after every statement (except after the last **end**, which has a dot after it). The only exception, as we shall see, will be that no semicolon must precede an **else**. Our convention will doubtless upset Pascal purists, but it has the merit that programs are easier to edit. A new statement can, for example, be inserted before an **end** without the need to append a semicolon to the statement that previously preceded the **end**.

Line-numbers

The last point is that Pascal programs do not contain line-numbers. In BASIC these are used for GOTOs and for editing. In Pascal, GOTOs are rarely used.

More to the point, and it is a big shock to someone brought up on BASIC, Pascal contains no editor. Moreover it has no built-in commands like RUN, SAVE, GET, OLD or NEW. Instead all of these are provided by an outside environment called an *operating system*. Operating systems are like governments. Nominally they are there for your benefit, but in practice they are large, cumbersome, hard to communicate with and, in general, an apparent hindrance to your progress. We discuss this in Chapter 3.

Pascal is not interactive. In BASIC you type lines one by one into the compiler (we use the word 'compiler' in this book to mean either a compiler or an interpreter). In Pascal you prepare a complete program using a separate editor – this will be explained later in case you have not encountered the idea before – and then feed it to a compiler. There are one or two interactive or semi-interactive Pascal compilers around, but they have not, as yet, become widespread.

Summary

We have so far encountered three concepts that have much more emphasis in Pascal than in BASIC. These are

- declarations
- data type
- structuring

We have also found that Pascal lacks the excellent features that BASIC has for editing, saving, restoring and generally managing programs.

Some friends

At this stage we should introduce two of our friends. Bill Mudd has been programming in BASIC for twenty years. One of his programs is 10,000 lines of BASIC, and it works – at least most of the time. His comments on the material so far presented in this book were not encouraging.

"Pascal looks to me like a language for head-in-the-clouds academics, who have never written a real program in their lives," he said. "You notice that the sample Pascal program is twice as long as its BASIC equivalent. I am particularly amused by all the useless things you have to type. You have to say **program** at the very start, just in case the computer thought you were preparing a shopping list. You then type several more lines of rubbish. When you finally get to the stage of typing the actual program you have to type **begin** just to warn the compiler that you have not changed your mind and decided not to write a program at all. Then you type much the same as in BASIC except that, because this would be too easy, you have to add a lot of extra semicolons and colons and parentheses and things."

Rather upset by Bill's uncouth attitude, we consulted our other friend, Professor Primple. The Professor is fanatically keen on Pascal. He has, like Bill, had twenty years of writing programs. He has written solutions to the eight queens problem in thirty different programming languages, has written recursive factorial functions in forty-three, and, best of all, has encoded Ackermann's function in seventy-two languages.

"Converting the heathen is always worth doing, I suppose," he told us, scratching his little beard in his characteristic way. "You will have to work hard to convert the savages from Basicland to the true good manners of Pascal. It is a pity you have started by oversimplifying many of the concepts, and, worse still, have encouraged the savages to sully the beauty of Pascal with redundant semicolons."

CHAPTER 2

The aims of Pascal

There is no such thing as a literal translation.

TEACHER OF FRENCH

Now we have given a hint of what Pascal programs are like, we shall, in this Chapter, discuss the aims of Pascal and some of its potential advantages.

History

One of the milestones in computing was the development of the Algol 60 language. Those of use who, in our schooldays, were tortured by history masters into remembering numerous dates regard the name Algol 60 with favour; the very name gives away its date, 1960. Algol 60 was developed by a committee of thirteen people, but, amazingly, it turned out to be a brilliant piece of work and has influenced the design of programming languages ever since. Algol 60 itself has not been used very widely, perhaps because it was ahead of its time, perhaps because there were not enough good compilers available, but its successors have swept the world. Algol 60 contains numerous good ideas, but one of the most important is *block-structure*. We shall discuss this concept later. Because it is such an important idea, Algol 60 and its successors have come to be called *block-structured language*s.

The language Pascal was developed in the late sixties by Professor Niklaus Wirth, of Eidgenössische Technische Hochschule, Zürich. It is a block-structured language that follows on from Algol 60; it both introduces new concepts and simplifies existing ones. By 1973 Pascal had a definitive form, and since then has achieved enviable success. Apparently, Professor Wirth had a map of the world on his wall, with a pin stuck into all the places that use Pascal. By now the map must be so perforated that it has fallen down in tatters. This success of Pascal, moreover, is not due to any high-pressure selling, or pushing by a powerful organization. People have chosen Pascal solely because they wanted it.

Nevertheless Pascal has not monopolized the field of block-structured languages. Other widely-used languages include C, BCPL, ADA and PL/I. Once you have learned Pascal you will find it relatively easy to switch into any other block-structured language, and vice-versa.

Specific design features

It is valuable at this point to emphasize two specific design features of Pascal which, because they do not apply to some of its competitors, have contributed to its success. The first is that Pascal has been designed with the problems of implementation in mind. The result is that Pascal compilers run relatively fast, and produce a program that also runs fast. Moreover Pascal compilers are not as huge and cumbersome as those for some other block-structured languages, and this accounts for the heavy use of Pascal on micros.

The second important design feature of Pascal is that it aims to be *lean and supple*. One of the greatest qualities of the language designer is to cut out ruthlessly every potential feature that is not worth its keep. The reward is a language that is easy to learn and to compile. It is no good, however, being ruthless unless the core features of the language are sufficiently supple that they can be bent to fill the holes left by the excisions.

It can be claimed – indeed we shall do so – that sometimes the wrong features have been cut from Pascal, but it is hard to quarrel with the aim of making a language small.

Definition of Pascal

In 1975 Springer-Verlag published the *Pascal user manual and report*. The authors are Kathleen Jensen and Wirth himself. The 'report' is a rather more formal definition of the material presented in the user manual. The term 'report' is not intended to mean that Pascal goes with a bang; instead it is a carry over from Algol 60, which was the report of a committee. We refer to the Pascal report many times in this book. If you are going to make extensive use of Pascal it is invaluable to have access to a copy of the Jensen & Wirth book; it is also a useful complement to the informal treatment that this book provides. If you are a person of refinement you should seek out an early edition of Jensen & Wirth, with its tasteful maroon and grey cover. If you are a glittering with-it life-style personality, you will doubtless prefer the edition with the shiny silver cover splashed with scarlet.

The Pascal report served as the definition of the language until an international standard was produced in 1981. The standard definition is very close to the Pascal report, and where there are differences most current compilers follow the report. The reason is that it takes many years for all the compilers used in the field to adapt to a new standard. We shall occasionally refer to the Pascal standard in this book, in situations where it differs from the report.

Variations in BASIC and Pascal

There are many different implementations of BASIC, and these vary quite considerably in the features they offer. Fortunately, however, most BASICs have a common core, and it is this core that forms the basis for explanations in the present book. Indeed there is an ANSI standard for minimal BASIC, which is now becoming widely observed. (There is standardization work on more advanced BASICs but, at the time of writing, this has had little effect in the field.)

There are, of course, many different implementations of Pascal too, but these tend to be similar to each other, as they are all based on the Pascal report. For any Pascal compiler that you plan to use, you should consult its particular user manual; we call this your *local manual*. Your local manual should contain a Section which defines where your compiler departs from the report or the standard. You will usually find that there are one or two extensions and perhaps some esoteric restrictions, but nothing very significant. As we have said already, this book is not concerned with unofficial Pascal extensions, however popular they may be, so you must depend completely on your local manual for descriptions of these.

When we say in this book that a feature is 'not in Pascal' or 'not in BASIC', we are speaking of definitive standard versions. You can doubtless discover individual Pascal or BASIC implementations that actually support such 'missing' features.

Portability

If your program is to achieve long life and success it must be *portable*. This means it must be easy to move the program from one machine to another, or between two different compilers on the same machine. If you avoid unofficial compiler extensions, you will find Pascal programs are quite portable. No-one who has moved a large program from one computer to another ever achieves this without any problems. However your problems with Pascal should be less than most.

In this respect BASIC is much worse than Pascal. BASIC systems vary hugely, and you will have correspondingly huge problems moving a large BASIC program from one system to another. Your only hope is to confine yourself to BASICs from one vendor, or to stick to ANSI standard minimal BASIC.

Method of implementation

If you know something about systems software you will understand that there is a difference between an *interpreter* and a *compiler*. If you then learn a lot more about systems software, you will find that the two concepts are not as different as you thought they were. We are not concerned with such subtleties in this book. That is why we describe any BASIC or Pascal system as a 'compiler', thus avoiding the clumsy repetition of 'interpreter or compiler'.

A program is processed by the computer in two stages. Firstly, the compiler converts your program into an internal form; if there are any syntax errors you are told of them. Secondly, if compilation is successful, the internal form of your program is run. These two stages are called *compile-time* and *run-time*. (The systems program that manages your program when it runs is called the *run-time system*.) The two stages are quite distinct in Pascal, though in some BASICs, particularly the very small BASICs that do not give syntax errors until a program is run, the difference is less obvious.

A few practical considerations

On a small computer your choice of language may be determined by severe practical limitations rather than higher-level aesthetic points. In such practical terms the comparison between Pascal and BASIC comes out as follows.

(1) *Size of store*   A Pascal compiler needs much more store than a BASIC one. As time goes by, and store gets ever cheaper, this consideration will become less important.

(2) *Speed of compilation*   Pascal is faster to compile than most block-structured languages, but it still tends to be slower than structurally simpler languages such as BASIC.

(3) *Speed of execution*   Pascal programs will not inherently run slower or faster than BASIC programs. Any differences stem from the quality of individual implementations.

To summarize, if your only concern in life is miserly use of store and machine time, then a switch from BASIC to Pascal is unlikely to help you.

Language issues

Let us assume, however, that you have wider horizons than extreme miserliness. We devote the rest of this Chapter to higher issues, and in particular to considering the potential advantages of Pascal over BASIC as a programming language.

BASIC has three great advantages. It is easy to learn, easy to use, and good for writing small programs.

When you have been programming for a while you discover that big programs are fundamentally different from small programs. By 'big' we mean several hundreds of lines. (A 'big' program to a professional programmer might be thousands or even millions of lines, but we shall be more modest.) When a program becomes big, one consideration comes to dominate all others: *the program must be easy to read and to understand, both by you and by others.* If this is achieved, almost every other desirable property follows. The program becomes easy to develop, both initially and when you make later additions. The program becomes easy to debug and to correct. The program becomes easy to share; a group of people can work together on a program, or you can write a program on your own and leave it for others to build on. It also becomes easier to make the program work correctly and reliably, and to have confidence in it. Finally there is one really devastating argument for readability: if your program is not readable no-one else will realize how superb your programming is.

If you write a small program that is hard to understand, this does not matter much. It will still be possible to follow what your program is trying to do. If you carry the same programming practices into a big program you will be totally sunk, because your program will become impossible for an ordinary human mind to comprehend. Pascal programs are inherently more readable than BASIC programs, and this is the prime reason why you should consider making a switch. You may not agree with this claim now, but you surely will when you have a proper understanding of Pascal. As a check, try to get hold of some Pascal programs (from a magazine or library, say) in a field that interests you, and, after you have got a feel for Pascal itself, investigate how readable the programs are.

Maintenance

The point about readability can be reinforced by considering what happens to a successful program after it has been written.

There has probably never been a program that has been used for many years without modification. Instead every program requires what is know as *maintenance*. Maintenance involves correcting bugs, and making small changes or additions. Such changes result from user demand or from changes in the hardware or software on which the program runs. For a typical production program the costs of maintenance are many times greater than the costs of writing the program in the first place. Thus the aim of a programming language should be to make a program easy to maintain, and if necessary this should be done at the expense of making the program harder to write in the first place.

If you work in a production environment there may be a clear point at which the maintenance stage begins. You write your program, and submit it to a process laughably called 'final testing'. When the test has been passed, the program goes out for others to use. After a very short time the users come back with bug reports or requests for changes, and from then on you sample the joys of maintenance.

If, on the other hand, you write programs just for your own use, and perhaps the use of a few friends and colleagues, the transition from development to maintenance is more gradual. You write an initial version, use it a bit, and then decide where further developments are to be made. You then produce a Mark 2 version and repeat the cycle. After a while you will find you are spending most of your time making changes and small modifications to existing pieces of program, rather than writing completely new routines. You have then entered the maintenance stage.

Maintenance may be done by the person who wrote the program, or it may be done by someone else. Actually there is very little difference between the two. We have all experienced the phenomenon of looking at one of our own programs, written a year or so previously, and thinking: 'What fool wrote this program? I can't understand at all what it is trying to do.' The program might just as well have been written by someone else.

Even if you are doubtful of our claim that readability makes programs easier to develop in the first place – and it is, of course, right to be suspicious of glib claims made in books – you must surely feel that all the advantages of readability are manifest during program maintenance.

Levels of readability

There are several possible ways of achieving readability. Important ones are

(1) making each statement easy to read
(2) structuring the program
(3) making the program relate closely to the problem
(4) imposing a discipline on programming style
(5) separating out those program elements that may require changing

We shall cover each of these in turn, relating them to Pascal's facilities.

Making statements easy to read

The biggest aid to making individual statements comprehensible is to use meaningful names for variables, subroutines, etc. Consider the three following equivalent statements in BASIC, Pascal and another language, COBOL

```
LET P3 = P1 + P2
totalpay := fixedpay + overtimepay;
ADD OVERTIME_PAY TO FIXED_PAY GIVING TOTAL_PAY.
```

The BASIC version is clearly the hardest to understand. The COBOL version is interesting in that it uses an English-like syntax. The COBOL language is much used by commercial programmers, and much despised (somewhat unjustly) by everyone else. Programs are so verbose that the equivalent of the BASIC program

```
PRINT 2 + 2
```

would take about twenty lines of COBOL. One of the original ideas behind COBOL was that programs should be understandable by accountants, managers, and so on, who know nothing about programming.

We have strayed into COBOL to raise some ideas about program syntax. Does the English-like notation help? Arguably it does not help in program maintenance because the maintainer is presumably already accustomed to the notation of his programming language. What is certain is that it *does* help if the objects being manipulated are given names that indicate their purpose.

Structuring

You cannot be in computing long without having the concept of 'structuring' thrust at you. Vendors of all kinds of software products claim them to be structured, and almost every article on software mentions 'structured programming'. Professor Primple alone has written 158 papers on the subject, but unfortunately we do not have space to reproduce them here.

All the hard selling of structuring has doubtless caused a lot of people to react negatively to the subject. This is, however, not really justified. Structuring is a *good guy* of programming. We shall call this good 'guy' Mrs. Buzz, after the queen bee, who, by imposing a cellular structure, manages to direct thousands of workers into building a coherent whole. The only way we can build really big programs, let alone maintain them, is to divide them up into simpler parts, which can be fitted together to make the whole. There are many different methods that come under the heading of 'structured programming'. The choice between the alternatives is not, perhaps, very crucial, but what is vital is that you follow the lead of Mrs. Buzz by having some coherent and practical overall philosophy for structuring what you do. Whichever philosophy you select, Pascal will provide tools to help you, though doubtless not everything you want.

Many programs are, of course, written by a team rather than a single person. In these cases not only must a programming language help the splitting up of a program into subprograms, but it must also make it easy for separate people to work on the subprograms without interfering with one another. Pascal has a concept of *local scope*, whereby variables can belong to one subprogram and be invisible to other subprograms.

Relating to the problem

If you program in BASIC the whole world needs to be represented by variables that are either of numeric or of string data type. However, many real-world problems do not naturally fit such data types. If the program is simulating a traffic light, for example, the data type naturally associated with this consists of the set of values red, amber and green (plus red-and-amber-together in some countries). If you represent these values as 1, 2 and 3 you lose something. This is so important that it brings us to introduce the first *bad guy* of programming. It is Mr. 869704, who encourages us to think in numbers when names would be better. As we shall see, Pascal has many ways of keeping Mr. 869704 at bay.

Imposing a discipline

One of the undeniable pleasures of programming is making clever or tricky use of a language in order to make the program extra small or extra fast. Sadly, such pleasures bring more than compensating agonies when, during the maintenance stage, a program needs to be modified.

Pascal attempts to impose a discipline on programmers by making tricks difficult or impossible, and, in some cases, by imposing a standard way of doing things. Disciplined programs are easy to understand.

If you have been used to great freedom, you will come to regard your Pascal compiler as a strict and fussy schoolmaster. You still have the chance to be creative, certainly, and you can still have fun, but you must play strictly by the rules.

The discipline has a purpose beyond making programs readable. It aims to make bugs rarer. Correcting bugs is a large part of the maintenance cost of a program and so the potential savings are enormous. If you follow a programming discipline, it will be much easier for you to verify that a program does what it is supposed to. It would be better still if there were automatic methods of verifying that programs work. Professor Primple has been working on such a system for many years. "I have a good method, which works especially well on the eight queens problem," he says, "but unfortunately my students and colleagues are not clever enough to understand it."

Given that we may not be up to using Primple's tools, we usually have to do our verification by laborious hand checking. A programming discipline is a godsend irrespective of how the verification is done.

We found Bill Mudd sitting at his terminal, and asked him about clever programming. "I am glad you asked me that," he said, excitedly. "This BASIC program I have here has two overlapping subroutines, one from line 1300 to 1721 and the other from 1529 to 1961. You see, one jumps over the other's RETURN. The really clever thing is that they are both half-embedded in a FOR loop which causes .... No, wait a minute. Come to think of it, it causes .... "

Separating out parts that may need change

One facet of a program that may well need changing is its constants. Paradoxically, constants often are not constant. Clearly the value of *pi* has had a good run as 3.14159 ..., and will doubtless continue its constancy. Likewise the chances of University lecturers being properly paid will remain at zero. However, programs often contain constants that represent such things as the size of an array, the width of a printed line, or the maximum number of records that can be processed. All these are likely to change when the program is being maintained, or if the program is run in a new environment.

Pascal has a means of declaring constants, so that it is easy to change them later. This also has the benefit that the meaning of an arbitrary constant is clarified – provided that the constant is given a sensible name.

The changing of constants is, of course, a minor part of the total task of program maintenance. However, Pascal's aids to Mrs. Buzz also help by making it easier for you to localize the effects of changes. It is, nevertheless, fair to warn you that you can overdo such efforts. As a general principle, if you put a large amount of effort into forecasting which parts of a program will change and which parts will not, you will be as successful as economists who try to forecast the nation's finances.

Errors

For most people, programming work is dominated by a single activity: debugging. This applies both during maintenance and during the original program development. Dealing with errors, or, more to the point, dealing with the possibility of errors is all-pervasive. Discipline, structuring and checking all help to reduce errors but do not eliminate them. (An exception arises with the programming activities of Professor Primple. In addition to his automatic verification tool, he has postulated a new structured programming discipline. It is covered in seventeen of his most recent papers, and is reported to eliminate errors, especially in the factorial function.)

Although most of us can never hope to eliminate errors, we can make realistic efforts to reduce their effects. The most important principle is that the earlier an error is found, the easier it will be to fix.

The following is a spectrum of times at which errors may be found

(1) before a program is submitted to the computer
(2) by the compiler
(3) immediately the error manifests itself during a run
(4) during a run, but after the true error has caused a number of subsequent side-effects
(5) by the answers being seen to be wrong
(6) by some subsequent disaster in the real-world, as a result of incorrect answers from the computer – our aeroplane with a fuel tank capacity of ten litres rather than ten million litres is involved in a nasty accident

The difference between (3) and (4) is best brought out by an example. If the error is an array subscript that is too large, this may be detected at the time the subscript is used. Some systems, however, do not detect such an error, but instead give the array element some gash value and blunder on. The error may then manifest itself some time later, when this gash value has gradually corrupted many other variables, and the program ends up taking, say, the square root of a negative number.

The aim of a programming language, and your aim as a programmer, should be to provide a series of safety nets to catch errors as early as possible. It is particularly valuable if your programming language makes it possible to catch at compile-time some potential run-time errors; Pascal provides help in doing this.

The overall term *security* will be used to cover techniques aimed at catching errors early. The security man is our second *good guy*. We shall call him Perkins, after an admirable man of this name. Do not expect Perkins to prevent all disasters; what he does achieve, and this is immensely valuable, is to make disasters less likely.

Evaluation

The above discussion has implied that, in all the five facets discussed, Pascal is great and BASIC is useless. That is much too simplistic a view.

For a start, most BASICs contain extensions that provide many of the facilities mentioned. Indeed the success of Pascal has caused many Pascal features to creep into BASIC. Nowadays almost every BASIC implementation supports more than ANSI standard minimal BASIC. These extensions are fine, but they suffer from a problem best illustrated by analogy.

You can start with a simple one-bedroomed house, and gradually extend it until you have a cathedral. However the end product is not likely to be a match for, say, Ely Cathedral or Chartres. Likewise add-on extensions to programming languages do not make a coherent and well-fitting whole; if the design aims are known at the outset, the chances of success are much greater. ("My guide book," said Bill, "says that Ely Cathedral was begun in 1083, extended by various people thereafter until 1322, when part of it fell down and was rebuilt in a different way.")

Over the past decades an important lesson has been learnt (by those who want to learn). This is that the jack-of-all-trades programming language is indeed the master of none. It is much better to have different programming languages – ideally lean and supple ones – to cover different applications. (If these different languages have a common core, all the better.) Each language has its own ecological niche. BASIC prospers where programs are small, storage is limited and users have no pretentions to be programmers. Pascal prospers for larger programs, on machines with more storage and where users, though not necessarily full-time programmers, nevertheless are prepared to put effort into programming. As we shall see, Pascal has its weaknesses too, and is superseded by other languages in many environments. With a huge amount of trouble you can grow grapes in the Arctic or keep penguins in the desert. Likewise you can nurture a programming language in an environment where it should die.

Humans and discipline

It is also possible to write good BASIC programs and bad Pascal programs. We all know people who can be guaranteed to write bad, unmaintainable, bug-ridden programs whatever programming language they use. Conversely, a good programmer will produce a reasonable product even if he has to use BASIC. You can write disciplined programs in BASIC, though the discipline must be self-imposed. The excellent book *The little book of Basic style* (Nevison, 1978) provides a basis for such a discipline.

Thus it can only be said that Pascal helps with the writing of disciplined and easily maintained programs, but human factors are at least as important as the choice of programming language. A good book on Pascal style and discipline is *Pascal with style* (Ledgard, Hueras & Nagin, 1979).

Changing the way you think

We now come to the most important point made in this book. *There is no point at all in writing a program in Pascal if you are going to continue to think in BASIC.* You can, indeed, write Pascal programs that are BASIC programs with a slightly different syntax, but you are not really using Pascal. What you must do is to change the way you think about solving programming problems. The mechanisms offered by Pascal, most of which we have not even mentioned yet, allow you to set about problems in radically new ways. Thus when we talk about 'learning Pascal' we mean a lot more than learning the grammatical and semantic rules of the language.

It is not, of course, easy to change your way of thinking. As we said in the Preface, it is *harder* to learn Pascal if you know BASIC than it would be if you did not know how to program at all. Professor Primple says that BASIC corrupts your mind. "The trouble with BASIC is that it is Wirthless," he declares, chortling away, while those in earshot inwardly groan.

Finally, let us remember the quote at the head of this Chapter. What the

French teacher was saying is that, if a translation is done word for word and phrase for phrase, it is not a proper translation at all. The literal translation is our second *bad guy* of programming, thus giving us two bad guys to counter our two good guys. This bad guy insidiously works away at our programs, introducing unpleasantness. His name is Frank Round; this name came out of an automatic language translating program, when trying to interpret 'open circuit'.

CHAPTER 3

Operating systems and editors

*Using [a well-known operating system] is
like trying to kick a dead whale along a beach.*

S C JOHNSON

We mentioned in Chapter 1 that to use Pascal you need to enter a world that you avoided or skirted with BASIC: the world of operating systems and editors. When this book is becoming particularly dreary or obscure it will be pleasant for you to break off and write some Pascal programs of your own. In order that you can do this we cover operating systems and editors now. If you already know about such things – and this may apply to the majority of readers – you can skip this Chapter, and all the more quickly sample the joys ahead.

Microcomputers and mainframe computers

The chances are that you have used BASIC on a microcomputer.

Pascal started as a language that ran on large and expensive *mainframe* computers, and only subsequently did it become available on microcomputers. A good proportion of the usage of Pascal is still on mainframe computers, though nowadays it is becoming harder to tell the difference between a mainframe and a micro.

There are, however, still differences in software philosophy. A mainframe computer usually tries to cater for a huge range of different users. The facilities are designed as much for an insurance company with twenty million policyholders as for individual users. The result is a huge hotchpotch which, as we shall see, can present learning problems. A micro, on the other hand, is geared much more for individual small users. Pascal may be similar on the two types of machine, but the surrounding facilities are likely to be totally different.

When you first use Pascal, it may be your first experience of mainframe computing. Even if you are continuing to use a familiar micro, you will still have a new experience as you need to adapt to using that micro in an unfamiliar way. The key point about Pascal is that programs are prepared in a completely different manner from BASIC, and we shall begin this Chapter by explaining the dichotomy.

Interactive and batch languages

BASIC is an *interactive* language. Pascal is a non-interactive or *batch* language. When you change from an interactive language to a batch language you will feel that you are taking a retrograde step, because preparing and compiling programs becomes a much more longwinded and tedious affair. Hence you must have confidence that Pascal is a *much* better language than BASIC if you are going to face up to the change. Once you get as far as running your program, there is not much difference: you can interact with a Pascal program just as you can with a BASIC one.

The difference between an interactive and a batch language is best explained first by analogy. An interactive language is like a supermarket, where all kinds of goods are gathered together under one roof. Not only can you buy any sort of goods, but you can wander randomly from one section of the supermarket to another, and, assuming you have not passed the check-out, you can change your mind about previous purchases. You may, for example, be in the wine section when you notice that you wrongly selected the variety of apple inaptly named Golden Delicious; if so, you can go back to greengrocery and remedy the blunder by taking, say, Lord Lambourne apples instead. Likewise if you decide you really must buy a few chocolate almonds, even though you originally passed them by with great forbearance, then you can go back and insert them into your basket.

In BASIC you can prepare programs, list them, save them, run them, retrieve old programs, and so on. This is done by a homogeneous set of commands within BASIC such as LIST, RUN, SAVE, etc. The analogy of using these commands is going into different sections of the BASIC supermarket. Moreover in BASIC you can easily *edit* (i.e. change) your program by inserting new lines among existing ones or by replacing existing ones – just like replacing the apples.

A good BASIC, running on a computer with a reasonable amount of storage, actually goes beyond our analogy. If you unknowingly type a wrong statement such as

LET A = B + / C

you are told of your error immediately; you don't have the problem of finding, after you have left the supermarket, that you picked up the wrong combination of goods.

The use of a batch language is more akin to a set of small specialist shops, scattered widely around a town. One is a baker, one is a butcher, one is a grocer, and so on. You go into the butcher's to buy some ham for your sandwiches. The butcher's ham is cut from the bone and tastes good, in contrast to the supermarket ham, which is little different from the plastic wrapping that encloses it. However if, while buying the ham, you suddenly remember that you did not get any bread while in the baker's, you have the inconvenience of going all the way back to the baker's to remedy your error. Furthermore, assuming you are from a civilized nation where all sandwiches contain butter, you always have to go to the grocer's too.

Using Pascal is akin to visiting a sequence of different shops. You start at the shop where you type in and edit programs. You then proceed to the compiler to check your program and prepare it for running. If the program is wrong, you go back to the edit shop; otherwise you go on to the shop for running programs. If the run produces incorrect results you go to yet another shop: one which helps you find out what went wrong.

Preparing a Pascal program

To be more specific, the precise sequence of preparing a Pascal program is as follows.

(1) You type the Pascal program into a file. This is done using an editor, which is suitable for both preparing new programs and changing programs that already exist in a file.

(2) Having left the editor, you feed your file to the compiler. This checks the program for errors in the use of Pascal. If there are any errors, you go back to stage (1) and use the editor to correct your program. If there are no errors, the compiler creates a new *object program*, which is a runnable version of your original source program.

(3) You run the object program.

(4) If your program stops because of an error, such as division by zero or an illegal subscript, you may have to enter a *debugger* to help you find out what went wrong.

We shall discuss all these four stages in more detail later in the Chapter.

The important point to note is that Pascal only defines what happens in stages (2) and (3). The editor is a completely independent program which is in no way tied to Pascal; the editor can just as well be used to edit programs in other programming languages, or even English text or numerical data. The debugger, again, is an independent program, though in some systems it is more closely tied to Pascal than the editor is.

Operating systems

The fundamental control of your computer and its peripherals rests with an *operating system*. The two most important components of an operating system are its *filing system*, which looks after your files, and its *command language*, which (among other things) allows you to select any of the above four stages of Pascal programming. Before discussing these two components in detail, we shall start by presenting a few facts.

(1) Operating systems and editors vary widely from machine to machine. They present radically different interfaces to the user.

(2) Some operating systems are huge – occupying many millions of bytes of code.

(3) Operating systems have been getting much easier to use in recent years. Those on micros are normally recent, and, by necessity, small; those on mainframes are often influenced by features that became obsolete in the sixties, but, for reasons of compatibility, still pervade the system. As a result, micro operating systems are often better, though less powerful, than their gargantuan relatives.

(4) Bigger operating systems allow many simultaneous users to 'time-share' the computer, whereas smaller systems only support one user at a time.

The current trend in computing is away from time-sharing and towards individual personal computers. There is, however, another trend away from the stand-alone personal computer and towards sets of personal computers connected together in a network. Computers on the network work independently, but can exchange files of information and can share expensive devices such as printers and type-setters.

Ideally an operating system should make the environment of operation invisible to the user. He should be unaware of any other users time-sharing his computer, and he should be unaware of whether a particular device is connected directly to his computer or accessed by a network – though when it is a question of picking up output from a printer it is nice to know where the printer is situated. Let us hope your operating system at least comes close to this ideal.

Filing systems

To the majority of users, the most important job done by an operating system is to support files; these files may be stored on one or more discs or the like. The following are the main facilities of a filing system.

- *Naming* If your backing storage can support more than one file, there must be a means of naming files so that you can specify which file you want. Usually a file name consists of an identifier such as PAYROLL or TEACH1, possibly followed by a cryptic *extension* telling you what type of file it is, e.g. PAYROLL.PAS may be a Pascal program, and TEACH1.BAS a BASIC program. Associated with one's files is a *directory*, which gives the names of all the files that exist on, say, a given disc.

- *Commands* The operating system provides commands for frequent filing operations, such as deleting, copying, or transferring to another medium (e.g. disc to tape).

- *Attributes* Files often have associated attributes. On a multi-user machine, some attributes may be associated with protection. You should be able to give your files attributes which prevent nosey friends from changing them or even, perhaps, looking at them at all. Other attributes may be associated with the permanence of a file. Some filing systems provide temporary files which are automatically deleted at the end of each session; this helps prevent the filing system becoming cluttered up with old rubbish. Finally, attributes may be associated with the *access method*. Files may be *random-access*, which means that you can pick out parts of the file in any order you want; this is like a reference book, which you do not normally read from beginning to end, but rather select entries you want to consult. Alternatively, files may be *serial*, which means that to reach any point you must start at the beginning and scan sequentially until you reach the desired point. There are many other types of access method in addition to these two, and this is one reason why some operating systems occupy millions of bytes; however, we shall not worry about them here. In practice most files are used as serial files, and, indeed, standard Pascal only supports serial files.

Command languages

In a sense, BASIC contains a command language: this consists of words such as RUN, SAVE and LIST. These are, however, so simple that you probably never thought of them as a language.

Operating systems provide command languages that generalize the commands found in BASIC, and provide other facilities as well. Indeed the command language is the fundamental interface between the user and the facilities at his disposal. Many operating systems support several programming languages, and commands are designed to be suitable for all languages. Therefore Pascal may be one of many languages, and commands may not have been designed with Pascal specifically in mind.

Some command languages are unbelievably complicated and verbose – whole books have been written about some of them. If you find the computer that you propose to use has a command language described in a 400-page user manual, then execute the following Pascal program

```
open(window);
repeat
    if strongenough(you) then
    begin
        pickup (manual);
        throwout (manual, window);
    end;
    reselect (computer);
until small (manual);
```

This program does, incidentally, introduce some Pascal concepts that we have not explained yet, but hopefully you have got the gist of what is intended.

Even with a simple command language, most programmers are forced into the defensive maxim: do not learn the whole language, just learn enough commands to get by. (You may already have done this if you have used BASIC under an operating system. With Pascal it will be necessary to extend your repertoire a bit.) Typical commands that you might need to know are as follows – remember, however, that command languages vary *immensely* and so your operating system may be nothing like this.

EDIT *filename*   enter the editor in order to work on the given file

PASCAL *filename*   compile the Pascal program contained in the given file

RUN   run the program most recently compiled

DEBUG   enter the debugger to throw light on what happened during the most recent run

Levels of communication

A point that causes initial confusion to BASIC programmers is that an operating system usually offers separate levels of communication. When BASIC asks you for a line, you can type a command or a line of program. When you are using an operating system and an editor to prepare a Pascal program, there may be three separate levels of communication.

(1) Initially you are in *command status* in the operating system. Here the only thing you can type is one of the commands in the command language, to tell the system what to do next. The command may be a simple self-contained one, like the deletion of a file. In this case the operating system obeys the command and returns directly to command status again. Alternatively it may be a command that passes control to some other system, such as the command EDIT to enter the editor.

(2) If you enter the editor, you go into *editor command status*. You must then type one of the commands provided by the editor, such as a command to insert some text. We discuss editing commands later.

(3) If you type a command to insert some text, you enter *data status*. You then type the appropriate text – in your case, a piece of Pascal program. At the end of the text you type a *data terminator* to return you to level (2).

When you have finished your editing you type a 'finish' command to return to the operating system command status (i.e. level (1)). At this point your Pascal program should be stored away in a file. You then type a command to cause your program to be compiled. We previously postulated this command as PASCAL *filename*.

Operating systems and editors are such an untamed bunch that everything we say about them, however general, has numerous exceptions. There are, for example, some systems that do not follow the above three-level hierarchy. There are editors where you distinguish commands from data by pressing the control key on the keyboard when you want to specify a command; otherwise everything you type is treated as data to be inserted. Other systems allow level (1) commands to be used at level (2). Nevertheless our three levels, even if only conceptual, may help to clarify your thinking.

Miscellany

Most modern operating systems, and their associated command languages, offer you the convenience of *device-independence*. This means that if a command produces some output, you can, according to your wishes, send that output to a file, to your terminal or to a line-printer. The workings of the command are independent of the device used. A similar mechanism applies to commands with associated input.

A command to compile or run a Pascal program may involve many input and/or output 'files'. A device-independent system is a great asset because it allows you, on occasion, to redirect these files.

In addition to a filing system and a command language, an operating system may have other facilities you need to know about. You may need to *log on* at the start by identifying yourself (name and secret password), and *log off* at the end. There may be accounting routines, which charge you for the use of the computer. There may also be utility programs, which perform useful tasks such as cleaning up files or preparing discs for use. If you are lucky, there will be a HELP command, which gives you advice when you get into trouble.

Finally, the most important thing to know before you start any programming is how to stop if things get out of hand, for example if your program goes into an endless output loop. Every operating system has a *break-in* key which can be used to abort the current activity. Normally the break-in key causes a return to command status within the operating system. Find out how to do a break-in before starting to run your programs.

Editors

Having given a brief description of operating systems, we shall now do a similar job for editors.

Editing is a simple concept. It involves creating and changing the contents of a file, and there are basically only three possible operations: deletion, insertion, and replacement. Editing is so simple, in fact, that any systems programmer can write an editor. Most have done so. The result is thousands of different editors, no single one of which has achieved domination.

People are extremely fussy about the editors they use. It is a characteristic of man – and this certainly includes woman – that as issues get more trivial, they stick ever more obstinately to their point of view. Thus people insist on using a particular editor because it uses R to mean *replace*, rather than another which, equivalently, uses C to mean *change*. Because of this prejudice some mainframe computers which support hundreds of users also support hundreds of editors.

If you have never used an editor before, beware. After you have learned your first editor you will never be the same extremely reasonable person again. (The BASIC system of using line-numbers to specify where a change is to be made, e.g. typing

100 LET X = 0

to replace an existing line 100, is in a sense an editor, so perhaps it is too late to warn you. Moreover some BASICs allow you to move a cursor on a screen to specify edits within a line.)

We shall explain some of the general features of editors. For details, and this is, as we have emphasized, where the trouble starts, you will need to consult your local editor manual.

Features of editors

The first thing an editor must do is to provide you with a way of specifying where in the file you wish to make a change. Some old editors required you to put your changes in the order in which they occurred in the file (e.g. if you had changed the tenth line you could not then change the ninth line), but few of these editors remain alive. Instead the editor makes the file to be edited seem like a random-access file, even if the underlying file is really a serial one. There are three basic ways of specifying the place to be changed.

(1) *Line counts* This is the least attractive method. You say something like "I want to change the fifty-ninth line." If the file to be edited is a long one then this method is impracticable unless you have a listing of the file with line counts marked on it. Note that these line counts are not like BASIC line-numbers, because the latter actually occur in the text of the program whereas our line counts do not.

(2) *By context* Here you have the concept of a current *point of scan*, which must be moved to the place where the change is to be made. To find a particular line you type a string of characters which, you hope, occurs uniquely on that line. The editor starts at the current point of scan and searches sequentially forwards (or, on option, backwards) until it finds a line containing the desired string of characters. It then displays this line, which itself becomes the current point of scan. You might, for example, ask the editor to find a line containing the string '$x + 3$;'. The editor would proceed from the current point of scan until it found such a line, which it would then display. The line might be

$count := x + 3;$

If this was the line you wanted, you would now be ready to make your change. If, however, it was before the line you wanted, you could continue searching for the same string, starting from this new point of scan.

(3) *By pointing a cursor* The most pleasant method of editing is to point at the place in your program that you want to change. You may already be familiar with this method from your BASIC system. It requires that you have a display with a movable cursor. The ultimate in editing is to have a special pointing device – one such is called a 'mouse' – that can be used to move the cursor across the screen; this is so good that even the most prejudiced will come round to it in the end. The alternative is to move the cursor around by depressing keys on the keyboard.

If you have a program of any size, it will not fit on a screen. Instead you can consider the screen to be a *window* that looks at part of your file. To move the window to another part of the file it may be necessary to use context editing. Alternatively, some really sophisticated editors allow you to indicate where in your file the window is to lie by moving the cursor down a scale that is displayed somewhere on the screen.

Editing commands

Once you have found the place in the program to be changed, you are ready to type an editing command to make the actual change. The most frequent commands are the fundamental ones: insert, delete and replace. These may work on whole lines of text, or on substrings within a line.

Over the years, the editor shop – to return to our earlier analogy – has expanded the range of goods it offers. Thus modern editors can also be used to do operations such as the following

- replace one string by another throughout a whole file. For example you could use the editor to replace the variable name *scnt* by *shipcount*

- insert some text stored in another file

- move text from one place to another

- search for all occurrences of a given pattern

This diversity gives editors a great chance to be different from one another, and they have taken full advantage of it.

Improved displays

When you are working with information on pieces of paper it is convenient to have several separate pieces in view at the same time. When working on a program, you may, for example, have the user manual open at a particular page so that you can relate it to a listing of your program and to a print-out of an error message that your program produced when it ran. Your eyes keep moving between the three pieces of paper.

Currently it is often hard to do the same thing when using a computer display instead of paper. However one of the most significant and happy trends of recent years, is the production of more powerful displays; these, coupled with sympathetic software, allow us to communicate more easily with computers. There are now systems where you can display several separate windows at once, and move them about on your display exactly like pieces of paper on a desk. Teitelman (1977) describes a superb system of this sort.

Perhaps surprisingly, displays on cheap personal computers are often more powerful than those connected to mainframe computers costing hundreds of times more. This is because expensive time-shared computers are too valuable to spend their time looking after a display. However this phenomenon is already disappearing as flexible networks of specialized computers become more common.

The reason that we have talked about displays in some detail is that, as editing becomes simpler, the differences between Pascal editing and BASIC editing may diminish. BASIC's system of using line-numbers for editing may fall into disuse if it is easier to edit a program by pointing at a window on a display.

Using a Pascal compiler

Having prepared or changed your program using an editor, you then enter the Pascal compiler by typing a command such as

PASCAL *filename*

Most Pascal compilers are completely non-interactive. You simply give them a file and then sit back and wait for the error messages to come out. You will get a lot more errors out of Pascal than you are used to from BASIC. This is for three reasons.

(1) Pascal is a more elaborate language.

(2) In Pascal, a single error may lead to a host of messages. If you forget to declare a variable, you may get an error message from every use of that variable. Moreover certain errors cause poor-quality compilers to get themselves in a mess so that they give several spurious errors following the real one. Thus you will sometimes find that when you correct one error, subsequent 'errors' may magically vanish.

(3) Because Pascal compilers are not interactive, it is easy to make the same mistake many times. At an elementary level you might forget to put a semicolon after any statement, and you would not learn your mistake until you compiled the whole program.

Do not be dismayed, therefore, when your first Pascal program, which occupies ten lines, generates twenty error messages.

A particular problem is caused by Pascal's facility for constructions that occupy several lines, for example

{ *a two-line*
comment }

If you forget the '}' character that terminates a comment, the compiler will search your whole program to find the next '}', ignoring everything it passes over. The result can be puzzling error messages. Similar problems can arise from missing string quotes or missing **ends**. Thus, if you find your error messages particularly enigmatic, look for these possibilities.

When you have reached the stage of producing a correct program, the

Pascal compiler will translate your program into an object program. This is what you RUN. You can run object programs as often as you like. Once you have a working program there is no need to compile it each time you want to use it, as almost every Pascal system provides a way of saving object programs in the filing system.

Running a Pascal program

We have assumed that to run a Pascal program you type the command

    RUN

(RUN – or EXECUTE, as some systems call it – might optionally be followed by the name of an object program if you wanted to run a program that was not the most recently compiled one.) Some 'compile-and-go' Pascals automatically start a run if compilation is successful, and, for these, the RUN command is unnecessary.

Running a Pascal program is like running a BASIC one, until things go wrong. When you have a run-time error or break-in, Pascal reveals its non-interactive nature: it (normally) gives you a fixed dump of the names of all your variables (excluding arrays and the like) and their values when the error occurred. It then gives up. You use the dump to figure out what went wrong.

Debuggers

Some operating systems provide interactive debugging systems, which can be used on Pascal programs. Several of these have facilities similar to those found in good BASICs, for example immediate statements.

Any decent debugging system should communicate with you in source language terms, i.e. in terms of the program you wrote rather than some internal representation that should not concern you. However there are still many indecent debugging systems around, so be prepared to have to learn about horrible internal details.

Sometimes a debugging system is integrated with the running of programs, and provides facilities like tracing, or executing your program one statement at a time.

These somewhat vague generalities are all we can say about debugging systems. Their diversity is so great that detail is pointless.

Special cases

As we have kept repeating in this Chapter, one of the joys, and the frustrations, of computer software is that both fundamental philosophies and low-level details vary widely. There are mavericks, and, over the years, some of these mavericks have been so successful that they have become regular establishment citizens.

Although BASIC is normally an interactive language and Pascal a batch language, there have been exceptions. The batch BASICs are like birds without wings, and will probably soon become extinct. The few attempts at interactive or semi-interactive Pascals are, on the other hand, more promising.

Moreover there are a few editors which are specially designed to deal with

Pascal programs and nothing else. Some of these are designed to help the user prepare syntactically correct programs. See, for example, COPAS (Atkinson & North, 1981) or *The Cornell program synthesizer* (Teitelbaum & Reps, 1981).

In spite of the potential importance of these mavericks, we shall not highlight them in the rest of this book, but shall continue to concentrate on the simplest and most frequent case.

An expert opinion

When we went to ask Bill Mudd about operating systems he was still at his terminal working on his clever piece of BASIC program. He had just replaced

    1096   GOSUB   4305

by

    1096   GOSUB   4605

but still the program did not work. Perhaps this accounts for his sour mood.

"With BASIC it is a trivial matter to change your program and re-run it," he said. "I have done fifty or so changes and re-runs just with this little piece of program. You are now asking me to waste five minutes ploughing through operating systems and editors to make each change."

"I do like one remark, though," he continued, as he made a further adjustment to his program. "The advice about hurling the manual out of the window if it is too big. I notice your book is already pretty big."

CHAPTER 4

Translation of BASIC concepts

*My friends, we will not **go** again or ape
an ancient rage,*

*Or stretch the folly of our youth to be the
shame of age.*

G K CHESTERTON

We have now finished with the background information, and the rest of the book is devoted to a fairly complete description of Pascal.

We do not, however, want this book to be a systematic catalogue of features. Instead we shall start with features you already know in BASIC, and build from there. Some new Pascal concepts will be introduced when they arise naturally in examples rather than in the position dictated, say, by the Pascal report.

In this Chapter we concentrate on individual statements, and the basic constituents that make them up, and in the next Chapter we go on to subroutines and functions. We have already covered, in Chapter 1, assignment statements and elementary input/output. (The simple assignment statement used in Chapter 1 is all that Pascal offers. There is no 'multiple-assignment' statement like the

$$\text{LET } A = B = 0$$

in some BASICs.)

If you wish to consult a precise syntactic definition of any Pascal feature, see Appendix C.

Spacing and comments

We shall start at the lowest level with the rules for laying out Pascal programs. As in BASIC, extra spaces may be freely added between the symbols of a program in order to improve layout. In Pascal you must insert a space when two words or numbers are adjacent, e.g. in

for $\uparrow$ *count*: $= y \uparrow$ **to** $\uparrow 6 \uparrow$ **do**

it is necessary to have at least one space in each of the four places marked by arrows. Spaces are not allowed within numbers or words.

As mentioned in Chapter 1, the end of a line is treated just like a space.

A comment, which in Pascal is enclosed between '{' and '}' as we have already seen, is also treated like a space. (You can use the symbols '(*' and '*)' as alternatives to '{' and '}' if the latter are not on your keyboard.) Comments can span any number of lines, and can occur within statements, e.g.

for *count* : $= y$ **to** $6 \{$ *stop at 6 because* ... $\}$ **do**

Names

When you name an object, such as a variable, you choose an *identifier*. An identifier is a letter followed by an arbitrarily long sequence of letters and/or digits. Lower case letters are normally treated as different from upper case letters. Sample identifiers are

$x, x1, Southampton6Spurs0$

Do not forget our advice to cast off the BASIC habit of using short names; instead choose meaningful names. Multi-word identifiers can be made more readable, if your compiler supports both upper case and lower case letters, by using upper case letters at the start of words, e.g. *ThreeWordName* is more readable than *threewordname*. (This book is, however, stingy in its use of upper case in Pascal, because of the convention of using upper case to represent BASIC entities.)

Some Pascal compilers take account of only the first eight characters of an identifier. If we had spelt *Southampton6Spurs0* as *Southampton0Spurs6* such compilers would not detect any difference.

Identifiers must not contain any spaces. ("I thought Pascal names were supposed to be meaningful," said Bill. "Ourtalkwouldnotbeverymeaningfulif-wecouldnotusespaces.")

All the words that form part of the syntax of Pascal (such as **var**, **for**, **to**, etc.) are called *reserved words*. These are the words which, for reasons of readability, are conventionally printed in bold face when Pascal programs are displayed in books. You cannot choose a reserved word as one of your identifiers. The complete list of these words that you must not use is

and	**downto**	**if**	**or**	**then**
array	**else**	**in**	**packed**	**to**
begin	**end**	**label**	**procedure**	**type**
case	**file**	**mod**	**program**	**until**
const	**for**	**nil**	**record**	**var**
div	**function**	**not**	**repeat**	**while**
do	**goto**	**of**	**set**	**with**

Do not bother trying to remember them all; if you happen to choose one of them as an identifier, Pascal will soon tell you.

Data types

Before considering individual BASIC statements, we shall roam in an area covered by Pascal and not by BASIC: *user-defined data types* and *subrange data types*. The purpose of doing this now is to make later examples more illuminating.

Pascal allows you to define your own data types. Doing this is not only a good practice; it is fun. There is a creative joy in achieving something that, in most languages, is impossible.

In order to provide some fodder for examples in this and subsequent Chapters we shall now define a completely new type of our own to supplement the types such as *integer* and *real* that are built into Pascal. This user-defined type is declared as follows

> **type**
>   *howout* = (*bowled, caught, stumped, runout, lbw*);

The declaration of **type**s comes just before the **var**s.

For the benefit of those from uncivilized lands where cricket is not played, we had better explain that the above user-defined type is a list of ways a batsman can be out. It could be used in a program to simulate cricket. To run such a program, the computer would, of course, need to be slowed down by many orders of magnitude in order to fit the proper pace of the game.

Each user-defined type is a sequence of identifiers representing all the constants of that type. Thus the constants of type *howout* are *bowled, caught, ..., lbw*. These constants are exact analogies of the constants 1, 2, 3, ... of the *integer* type. The purpose of a user-defined type is to make the program more readable. Once you have declared a type you can then define variables to be of that type. For example you can declare a batsman

var
    batsman: howout;

The variable *batsman* can take on one of our set of values – indeed these are the only possible values it can take. Thus we can say

    batsman : = bowled;

This is a lot better than the style that Mr. 869704 forces on BASIC programmers, which is to represent *bowled, caught*, etc. as some arbitrary numbers.

Note that Pascal's user-defined types are *completely* different from integers, in the same way that strings are different from integers in BASIC. You cannot therefore say *bowled* + 1 or set a *batsman* to zero.

(In the Pascal literature, user-defined types are often called *scalar* types or *enumerated* types.)

Subrange types

Pascal also allows you to define a data type that is a subrange of an existing data type. For instance the **type** declaration

    positiveinteger = 1 .. *maxint;*

declares *positiveinteger* to be a new type which is a subrange of the existing *integer* type. The subrange starts at the integer 1 and goes up to *maxint*, which is a built-in Pascal constant representing the largest integer that your compiler will support. Thus our subrange type, as its name says, consists only of positive integers. If a variable of this type were assigned a negative or zero value it would be an error.

Other examples of subranges are

{ *The type below consists of the 11 possible values:* −5, −4, ..., 4, 5 }
    smallinteger = −5 .. 5;

{ *The type below excludes lbw, which is often disputed* }
    certainlyout = *bowled .. runout;*

Subranges have three main uses. Firstly, and most importantly, they can be used to give better security to a program. If Perkins knows that a positive integer is expected in a given place, he can immediately weed out a negative integer as a rogue. Secondly, subrange types can be used by a compiler to save storage; a compiler could, if it liked the idea, store our *smallinteger*s in a single byte, or even in four bits. Thirdly, subrange types are invaluable for array bounds, as we shall see.

Subrange types are *compatible* with their 'host' types. This means, for example, that everywhere you can use an integer variable you can also use a *small-integer* or *positiveinteger* variable. (There is one minor exception: this will be discussed when 'variable parameters' are introduced in the next Chapter.)

As an example of Perkins' work with subrange types, consider the statement

$$p := q - 10;$$

where p is a *positiveinteger* and q is a *smallinteger*. The value of q cannot be greater than 5, and therefore $q - 10$ must be negative; thus the effect of the statement must be to try to set p to a negative value, so Perkins gives an error message. Some compilers are clever enough to catch such errors when a program is compiled, thus avoiding the overheads of run-time checking. Nevertheless in most cases the check must be done at run-time; for example in the statement

$$p := q;$$

a check must be made at run-time to ensure that the value assigned to p is positive.

In a sense a subrange type is a user-defined type – after all, the user defines it. However it is based on an existing type, and we have reserved the term *user-defined type* for types which, like *howout*, are defined from scratch.

Declarations

All Pascal objects, apart from numeric and string constants, are represented by identifiers. In every case there must be a declaration of what the identifier means. Thus in

type
    $t = (ct1, ct2);$
var
    $v1$: *integer*;
    $v2$: t;

The identifier t is declared to be a type; $ct1$ and $ct2$ are declared to be constants of type t; $v1$ and $v2$ are variables. (The former is an integer and the latter is of type t.) With one exception, to be explained later, all identifiers must be declared before they are first used.

If you are declaring several variables of the same type you can combine them to avoid repeating the type. Thus

    $x1$: *integer*;
    $x2$: *integer*;
    pig: *integer*;

can be written

    $x1, x2, pig$: *integer*;

Built-in functions

Pascal, like BASIC, supports a set of built-in functions, and these functions have identifiers as their names (e.g. *sin*, *cos*). Unlike reserved words, you can use these names for your own identifiers. Thus your best-selling porno program can have a variable called *sin*, though the program could not then use Pascal's *sin* function – but doubtless it would not want to anyway. (Similar rules apply to names of built-in types, such as *real* and *integer*, and built-in constants, such as *maxint*.)

Most of the built-in functions in BASIC have equivalents in Pascal, though several have different names. The following list gives translations.

BASIC	*Pascal*
ABS	*abs*
ATN	*arctan*
COS	*cos*
EXP	*exp*
LOG	*ln*
RND	non-existent
SGN	non-existent
SIN	*sin*
SQR	*sqrt*
TAN	non-existent

All the above Pascal functions take a real argument and return a real result, except for *abs*, which can be used with integers or reals. The BASIC function INT is similar to Pascal's quaintly named *trunc* function (the name is 'truncate' truncated); *trunc* only differs from INT if the argument is negative: *trunc* (-3.2) is -3 whereas INT(-3.2) is -4. The *trunc* function always gives an integer result.

Some extended Pascals fill the gaps represented by 'non-existent' in the above table.

The worst news for the BASIC programmer is that Pascal has a function *sqr* which means the square of its argument rather than the square root. The evilly-named Mr. Sqr is a real bad guy. If you build a bridge on the basis of some Pascal calculations, and the bridge falls down, check to see if you have let Mr. Sqr into your program when you really wanted *sqrt*.

Ironically, *sqr* is the only extra goody you get among Pascal's standard arithmetic functions.

Constants

Numeric constants are identical in BASIC and Pascal, except that in Pascal you must always have at least one digit before a decimal point. Thus BASIC's .1 becomes Pascal's 0.1.

Expressions

By and large, arithmetic expressions are much the same in Pascal and BASIC. Such differences as there are concern the difference between integer and real types, and the use of the exponentiation operator.

You can mix integers and reals in a Pascal expression, and you get the results you expect. Thus if you add an integer to a real you get a real. The main thing you must not do is to assign a real value to an integer variable – instead you can use the *trunc* function to convert the real to an integer before assigning it. The division operator '/' always gives a real result; if you have integer operands and want an integer result you should use the **div** operator. This truncates its result to the integer part. Thus

7 **div** 4 is 1
5 **div** 4 is 1
5 / 4 is 1.25

The operator **mod**, which, like **div**, works with two integer operands, gives the remainder when the first operand is divided by the second. Thus

5 **mod** 4 is 1
7 **mod** 4 is 3

If you try to write

$x \uparrow y$

in Pascal it will not work, because Pascal has no exponentiation operator at all. What you need to do, is to write

$exp(y * ln(x))$

However, if the power is an integer, you can find some more efficient way. Thus BASIC's

X↑4

can be written in Pascal, using the wicked *sqr* function,

$sqr(sqr(x))$

Given that the *exp* and *ln* functions are slow to execute, whereas *sqr* is relatively quick, the above runs much faster than the more general form. In fact the very purpose of the lack of exponentiation in Pascal is to make you think about what you really want, and then to use the most efficient method.

IF statements

We can now consider individual BASIC statements, and the first that we shall take is the IF statement.

If you are used to writing IF statements such as

IF X = Y THEN 500

you will need to change your way of thinking when you come to Pascal.

The problem is not the *relational expression* which comes between the IF and the THEN (e.g. X = Y above), but what comes after the THEN.

To start with the easy part, BASIC's relational expressions are the same in Pascal, though you can often improve your program by using Pascal's more advanced facilities in this respect. Actually Pascal allows a more general construction called a *Boolean expression* where BASIC allows a relational expression. We shall discuss this construction later – think of it for the time being as a relational expression.

The *relational operators*, i.e.

$$=, <>, >, >=, <, <=$$

are written identically in BASIC and Pascal.

Now for the big difference. Pascal supports two forms of **if** statement. They are written

> **if** *< Boolean expression >* **then** *< statement >*

and

> **if** *< Boolean expression >* **then** *< statement >* **else** *< statement >*

The notation used above should be obvious: *< x >* means any instance of the class *x*. The statement following the **then** is executed if the Boolean expression is true, and the statement following the **else**, if there is one, is executed if the Boolean expression is false.

Do not forget that in every situation in Pascal where a statement is required you can supply several statements enclosed by **begin** and **end**. There is one special rule to observe about the syntax of **if** statements: *never* put a semicolon before an **else**. Otherwise extra semicolons, within reason, do not matter. ("I told you that you made an appalling mistake back in Chapter 1, when you told them to put a semicolon on the end of every statement," repeated Professor Primple, in a tone that indicated no argument to the contrary would be tolerated.)

The following is an illustration of a short piece of BASIC program and its equivalent in Pascal.

```
100  IF X > Y THEN 150
110  LET P = 0
120  GOTO 200
150  LET P = 1
160  PRINT "X IS GREATER THAN Y"
200  ...
```

```
if x < = y then
     p: = 0 { no semicolon here! }
else
begin
     p: = 1;
     writeln(' x is greater than y');
end;
```

It is worth re-emphasizing here that Pascal programs can be laid out in any way you like. Arguably, the layout we have used above makes the meaning clear, but there are numerous alternatives – including squashing everything into one or two lines.

A second and simpler example shows an **if** without an **else**. In BASIC this is

```
100  IF P = 0 THEN 120
110  LET Q = 1
120  ...
```

whereas the equivalent Pascal is

if $p <> 0$ **then**
   $q := 1;$

In many BASICs you can write something very similar to the above Pascal statement. (Indeed some BASICs offer the full IF ... THEN ... ELSE of Pascal.)

The essence of the Pascal **if** is to think positively. In other words you think of what you wish to do when the relation is true; in minimal BASIC, on the other hand, you frequently think in terms of what you skip over, i.e. do *not* do, if a relation is true.

Backward jumps

Often the line-number following a BASIC THEN specifies a backward jump rather than a forward one; such IFs cannot be translated into Pascal in the way shown above. They apparently need a GOTO.

This leads us to an important point: GOTOs are *bad guys* of programming. They are all the more insidious because they appear so simple and harmless. At least, that is what Professor Primple says. Academics uncovered the wickedness of the GOTO in the sixties, and nowadays the evil fellow is never even mentioned in centres of learning and erudition. In the seventies others followed the academic lead, and hard businessmen became convinced that GOTO was losing them money, and hence should be fired.

When you write in Pascal you should banish GOTOs from your mind. A backward GOTO represents part of a loop, and should be expressed using the looping constructs that we shall shortly introduce. A forward GOTO can normally be expressed in terms of **if** statements.

If you take an existing BASIC program and translate it to Pascal, you will find it hard to get rid of the GOTOs. You can only eliminate GOTOs by rethinking your algorithms in terms of higher-level constructs. If you have been using GOTOs for years, it is a hard adjustment to make, but try nevertheless. You will soon find that doing without GOTOs is reasonably painless. Perhaps an apt analogy is switching from typing with one finger that has to jump all over the keyboard to typing properly with a unified approach using all the ten separate facilities that your hands provide.

The advantage of eliminating GOTOs is that programs become more readable. It is also easier to check that programs do not contain logical errors.

GOTO statements

"Wait a minute," said Bill, with a triumphant smile. Rather surprisingly, he brought out a Pascal book that was hidden under a masterpiece entitled *Intergalactic warfare programs*. "I see you can write GOTOs in Pascal. In fact they are the same as BASIC except that there is a lot of redundant rubbish to specify, as usual. You can write

goto 10;

and then you can write

10:

in front of the statement you want to go to. You can use any label numbers you like; they do not have to be in any sort of order. The only nuisance is at the very beginning of the program – after that useless **program** line – you need to write a line of the form

label 10, 20, 40, 67, ... ;

listing all the labels you have used."

To be truthful, **goto** is occasionally useful in Pascal, though Professor Primple denies it. Indeed Pascal compilers are usually themselves written in Pascal, and some of these use **goto**s. The **goto** is especially useful in error situations where the natural action is to jump out of the current flow of logic, and proceed to some entirely separate action. However we stand by our advice that it is best to try to banish **goto**s from your thinking, and only introduce them as a last resort.

FOR statements

We have already seen simple examples of Pascal's **for** in Chapter 1. In BASIC, the *controlled variable*, i.e. the variable whose name follows FOR, must be of numeric data type. In Pascal, as we shall see, it can be of other data types, but if it *is* numeric it has two severe restrictions. ("You mean 'too severe restrictions'," said Bill.)

The first restriction, which we have mentioned already, is that the controlled variable must not be real. The reason for this restriction is that real arithmetic is inexact. A BASIC statement such as

FOR K = .1 TO 1 STEP .1

is therefore playing with fire. If adding together ten instances of .1 comes out as 1.00000001 rather than 1, then the loop is only executed nine times, rather than ten as intended.

The second restriction comes from one facet of Pascal's leanness: there is no equivalent of BASIC's STEP. Instead the step must be either 1 or −1. In the latter case you write **downto** in place of **to**, e.g.

```
for k := 1 to 10 do
for k := 10 downto 1 do
for index := i + 1 to abs (q) do
for index := last downto first do
```

In the last two examples the values of i, q, *last* and *first* are taken at the start of the loop, and any changes of their values within the loop have no effect on the **for**. BASIC has a similar rule. You should not change the value of the controlled variable within the loop, nor should you assume that after

```
for k := 1 to 10 do { ... };
```

has finished, k will necessarily have the value 11.

Do not be too downhearted by these restrictions as they are more than compensated for by two other looping statements that Pascal provides. The first is the **while** statement. This has a syntax similar to an **if** statement without an **else**; the difference is that an **if** causes a statement to be executed once if a condition is true whereas a **while** causes a statement to be repeated continually while a condition remains true. The following example illustrates this.

```
count := 1;
{ .

  . }
if count < 11 then
begin
    writeln (count);
    count := count + 2;
end;
while count < 11 do
begin
    writeln (count);
    count := count + 2;
end;
```

The **if** prints the value 1 and sets *count* to 3. The **while** loop is executed four times. The variable *count* starts at 3, as a result of the preceding **if,** and is incremented by 2 each time round the loop. When *count* reaches 11 the condition on the **while** becomes false and the loop stops. Thus the values printed in the loop are 3, 5, 7 and 9. The above **while** also shows how the equivalent of a **for** with a step of 2 can be programmed.

The second extra looping construct is the **repeat**. The following example shows its syntax.

```
count := 3;
{ .

  . }
repeat
    writeln (count);
    count := count + 2;
until count >= 11;
```

The meaning is obvious. The **repeat** loop is similar to a **while** loop except that the test comes after, rather than before, the loop. The above **repeat** example is, in fact, another way of expressing our previous **while** example. Note that it is a quirk of Pascal's syntax that you do not need to have a **begin** and **end** round the body of a **repeat** loop, even if it involves more than one statement. If you find this rule confusing, always put the **begin** and **end** in; they will do no harm.

All Pascal's looping constructs can be nested, just like BASIC's FOR statement.

If your thinking is controlled by BASIC, your mind will equate a loop with a variable taking a sequence of values as in a FOR statement. If you switch to Pascal, you must broaden your mind and think 'loop' when you previously thought 'backward GOTO'. Such loops are naturally written using **while** and **repeat**. To start with, you will doubtless first try a **while** and then change it to a **repeat** or vice-versa. After repeating this for a while, you will get a feel for which construct to use; the key difference is that a **repeat** loop is always done at least once whereas a **while** loop is not. To bring this out, consider what happens to our previous examples if *count* starts with the value 100 rather than 3; our **while** loop does not then print anything, but our **repeat** loop prints 100.

To summarize, if you are used to one tool and are presented with a set of three tools to replace it, you will need some time to adapt. As looping is often the most important feature of a program, and because Pascal's three tools are so much better than BASIC's one, it is worth making the effort to adapt properly.

Sounds, pictures

Having discussed looping at length, we now come to a topic that can be dismissed with brevity.

Many BASICs have facilities for drawing pictures and making sounds. These are totally absent from standard Pascal, and are only just finding their way in as Pascal extensions. Likewise for PEEK or POKE.

"There is a simple rule concerning Pascal," said Bill. "If it's fun to do you can't do it."

"I wonder what the best-selling porno program is like in Pascal, without any graphics," he added, smirking.

ON statements

The BASIC ON statement

```
100  ON X GOTO 110, 150, 200

110  REM CASE WHEN X = 1
120  LET Y = 3
130  GOTO 500

150  REM CASE WHEN X = 2
160  PRINT Y
170  LET Y = 7
180  GOTO 500

200  REM CASE WHEN X = 3
210  LET Y = 29

500  ...
```

is translated into a Pascal **case** statement of form

```
case x of
   1:
      y := 3;
   2:
      begin
         writeln(y);
         y := 7;
      end;
   3:
      y := 29; { strictly speaking, this semicolon should be omitted }
end;
```

The numbers 1, 2 and 3 are *not* ordinary labels. Bill cannot GOTO them. They are called *case labels*, and are constants of the same data type as *x*, i.e. integer in our case.

The **case** statement is a whole lot better than BASIC's ON statement. Any possible values of *x* can be used as case labels, and you can put a list of case labels, separated by commas, on a single case, for example

23, 19, 46: *y* := 9; { *multiple* **case** *labels* }

Case labels can be in any order; you must not, of course, use the same case label more than once within the same **case** statement.

Mrs. Buzz is greatly helped. The overall structure, with the different cases nicely separated out, aids readability.

The *case selector* (*x* in our example) can be any expression; it can yield an integer value, or, as we shall see later, values of other types such as character or *howout*. (In these situations the case labels would not be numbers. For *howout*, for example, they would be *stumped, bowled*, etc.) This adds greatly to the flexibility of **case** statements.

The one problem with **case** statements is the error case. What if *x* had the value 4 in our example, and there was no case label 4? Unfortunately Pascal does not define what happens in this situation; a good compiler will give you an error message, but a bad one might perform some random action.

BASIC statements with no Pascal equivalents

A number of BASIC statements have no equivalent in Pascal.

The END statement has no equivalent, except perhaps the dot at the very end of a Pascal program.

A Pascal program automatically stops when it reaches the end. Most Pascal implementations offer a statement

halt;

which is the equivalent of the BASIC STOP, but this is not completely standard.

The RANDOMIZE statement, and the RND built-in function, are likewise not in the Pascal report, but many Pascal implementations offer similar facilities.

The DATA, READ and RESTORE statements have no equivalent in Pascal. All input must be done in a manner similar to using BASIC's INPUT statement. DATA is very useful in BASIC for initializing tables. Doing the same thing in Pascal is much more tedious; you need to write explicit assignment statements, or input the values from a file.

The hideous OPTIONBASE statement in BASIC is submerged in the Pascal equivalent of the BASIC DIM.

Constants, types and declarations

Finally, it is useful at this point to introduce a Pascal facility heralded in Chapter 2: the ability to make constants easy to change. This is done in Pascal by giving the constant an identifier as a name, and equating this to the value of the constant. All these constants are grouped together into a **const** section that comes at the very start of your declarations ("but after the labels," said Bill), so that they are easy to find if they do need changing. Sample constant declarations are

```
const
    linewidth = 72;
    maximumrepeats = 20;
    assentcharacter = 'y'; { constants can be single characters }
```

These names can then be used anywhere in your program where you would have used the constant.

As well as giving names to constants you can give names to types. Because it is sensible to give every type a name, we gave names to all the types we introduced earlier in this Chapter, such as *howout* or *smallinteger*. (Later on we shall introduce many other types, such as arrays and records; these too can be named.) Names you define yourself can be used in a similar way to Pascal's built-in type names, such as *integer* and *real*. Actually you do not need to give types a name but can write them explicitly after a variable declaration. Thus

```
type
    digit = 0..9;
var
    mynumber: digit;
```

can be written

```
var
    mynumber: 0..9;
```

Nevertheless we still stand by our advice to give types a name, although you will not understand the reason why until later on in this book. (On occasions we shall not follow our own advice; the excuse for this is to make examples self-contained, and not dependent on a separate **type** declaration.)

We have now mentioned four possible different sections of declarations. The following example summarizes them – giving one declaration in each section – and shows their ordering.

label
   200;

const
   linewidth = 40;

type
   lineposition = 1 .. *linewidth*;

var
   linepointer: lineposition;

{ *Now come the procedure and function declarations — see next* **Chapter** }

begin
{ *The executable statements start here* }

Any section that you do not use can be omitted. It is easy to remember the ordering. Labels come first so that Primple can immediately see if you use **goto**s, and, if you do, he does not have to look at anything you have written. For the rest, the **const**s might be needed by the **type**s, and the **type**s will certainly be needed by the **var**s, as our example shows; this fixes the ordering.

CHAPTER 5

Subroutines
and functions

It makes the going easy, and the coming back.

ADVERTISEMENT FOR RAILWAY RETURN FARES

Basic concepts

One of the best ways of dividing a large program into manageable units is by means of subroutines. The simple GOSUB and RETURN facility provided by minimal BASIC is tolerable for small programs, but becomes totally inadequate for larger programs. (That is why several BASICs offer extended facilities.)

Pascal supports both functions and subroutines – the latter are called *procedures*. Pascal functions have some similarity to BASIC functions, particularly to the multi-line functions offered by some BASICs. A Pascal procedure is very similar to a Pascal function; it can be thought of as a function that does not return a result. It is, therefore, more like a BASIC multi-line function than the GOSUB and RETURN mechanism.

We shall start by giving an example of a BASIC multi-line function that finds the greatest common divisor of two integers X and Y. The function is taken, by permission of John Wiley and Sons, from the fine book on BASIC by Kemeny & Kurtz (1980).

```
110   DEF FNE (X, Y)
120       REM THIS USES AN ALGORITHM DUE TO EUCLID
130       LET Q = INT(X/Y)
140       LET R = X − Q*Y
150       IF R = 0 THEN 190
160           LET X = Y
170           LET Y = R
180           GO TO 130
190       LET FNE = Y
200   FNEND
```

The equivalent Pascal function is as follows

```
function GreatestCommonDivisor(number1: positiveinteger;
                              number2: positiveinteger): positiveinteger;
{ This function returns the greatest common divisor of number1
  and number2. The method used is Euclid's algorithm. }
var
    remainder: integer;
begin
    repeat
        remainder := number1 mod number2;
        if remainder < > 0 then
        begin
            number1 := number2;
            number2 := remainder;
        end
    until remainder = 0;
    GreatestCommonDivisor := number2; { the result of the function }
end; { GreatestCommonDivisor }
```

The above is a declaration of the function and is placed with the other declarations. Specifically, function and procedure declarations are placed after the variable declarations, i.e. after the section headed by **var**.

A Pascal function is called in a similar way to a BASIC one, e.g.

$x := y + GreatestCommonDivisor(y + 6, q);$

Arguments and parameters

If you write in BASIC

DEF FNX(P) = ...

PRINT FNX(L + 9), FNX(Q9)

the variable P used in the definition of FNX is called the *parameter*, and the expressions such as L + 9 and Q9 that are used in calls of FNX are called *arguments*. The parameter is a kind of dummy. Each time the function is called, the value of the parameter is set to the value of the corresponding argument.

Pascal works much the same, except that different terminology is used: arguments are called *actual parameters*, and parameters are called *formal parameters*. One is, of course, free to call things what one likes, and it seems best, in this book, to keep to the simple terminology of BASIC.

Applying this terminology to *GreatestCommonDivisor*, the identifiers *number*1 and *number*2 are parameters, and in our sample call $y + 6$ and q are the arguments corresponding to *number*1 and *number*2 respectively.

Just to be fair, we shall favour Pascal by using its convention of calling a subroutine a procedure.

In Pascal, unlike BASIC, each procedure or function can have as many parameters as you like. Thus, one function might have no parameters and another might have five. If this is so, you must never supply an argument when you call the first function, and you must always supply five arguments when you call the second function. At the call of a function, the argument is assigned to the parameter, and so the two must be compatible in type. The rules are just the same as for a normal assignment statement. Hence an integer argument can match a real parameter but not vice-versa. Identical rules apply to the built-in functions; thus, for example, although *sqrt* wants a real argument, it will actually accept an integer and convert it to a real form behind the scenes.

Points to note

There are many points to note about the *GreatestCommonDivisor* function. The first is that the function looks exactly like a complete Pascal program (except for the ';' rather than '.' after the final **end**). This is a deliberate and happy design feature, as functions and procedures are a means of splitting a program into smaller subprograms. It is convenient to regard a program as a procedure; a run of the program is equivalent to a call of this procedure. The program has as its parameters the files that are used to communicate with the outside world. This is why the first line of a program is

>**program** *progname*(*input, output*);

The names *input* and *output* are internal Pascal names for the default input and output files. We discuss this further in Chapter 9. The executable part of the function is enclosed by a **begin** and **end**. This looks like a compound statement, but you still need **begin** and **end** even if the function consists of a single statement.

The second point is that declarations are local to the function. This is a really important idea, and we devote a lot of attention to it later in this Chapter.

The third point concerns the purpose of the heading line

>**function** *GreatestCommonDivisor*(*number*1: *positiveinteger*;
>   *number*2: *positiveinteger*): *positiveinteger*;

This heading, which we have split over two lines because it is rather long, first gives the name of the function. You do not have to use names as long as *GreatestCommonDivisor*, but long names, up to a point, aid readability. The function name is followed, in parentheses, by the declarations of its parameters. These declarations are written exactly like the list of declarations you write in the **var** section; note that you do not put a semicolon after the last declaration. Our two parameters, *number*1 and *number*2, are both of type *positiveinteger*, the subrange type we defined in the previous Chapter. We could, in fact, have shortened these declarations to

>(*number*1, *number*2: *positiveinteger*)

The final element of the heading gives the data type of the result of the function. In our example this too is a *positiveinteger*. (It is a quirk of this example that *positiveinteger* occurs three times; in general, as we shall see, these can be three different types.) The general form of a function heading is therefore

>**function** <*name*> (<*list of parameters*>): <*type*>;

For functions with no parameters, the parenthesized list of parameters is omitted.

All the data types used in function declarations must be names of types. You cannot, for example, write an explicit 1..10. This was one reason for our earlier advice to give a name to any type you define.

The reason we use *positiveinteger* rather than *integer* as the data type of the two parameters is to help Perkins. If the function is called with a negative or zero argument, Perkins can point out the mistake straight away. (Actually, if we had allowed any integer as argument, the function would only fail when the second argument was zero – this is because **mod** would try to divide by zero. The function would return a result if either argument was negative, though it is questionable if this result would be what the user wanted. It is like a customer ordering roast beef and custard in a restaurant; the result can be achieved but an attentive waiter would question the choice.)

The advantages of our also using *positiveinteger* rather than *integer* as the data type of the result of the function are not so striking. However it does provide some extra information for Perkins, and for any reader of the program. The more Perkins knows, the safer you are.

The two following examples of function declarations should throw more light on function headings.

type
    posor0integer = 0..*maxint*; { *a positive or zero integer* }

var
    readcount: integer; { *count of the numbers read by the readcubed function* }

{   .
     .
     . }

function *power*(*x: real; k: posor0integer*): *real;*
{*This function returns the kth power of x*}
var
    result: real;
    index: integer;
begin
    result := 1;
    for *index* := 1 **to** *k* **do**
        result := *result* ∗ *x;*
    power := *result;*
end; { *power* }

function *readcubed: real;*
{ *This function reads a real number and returns its cube.*
 It also counts the number of numbers read }
var
    inputnumber: real;
begin
    read(*inputnumber*);
    readcubed := *power*(*inputnumber*, 3);
    readcount := *readcount* + 1; { *count the numbers read* }
end; { *readcubed* }

The *power* function shows parameters of different types from one another.

The *readcubed* function shows a function without any parameters. It also shows that a function can call other functions, and can refer to a variable declared outside itself (*readcount* in the above example). All these points have exact parallels in BASIC.

These two functions also illustrate a good programming practice: put a comment at the start of a function declaration to explain what it does, and, after the **end** of a function, put a comment to give the name of the function that is ended.

The workings of the function

If you now look at the workings of our original *GreatestCommonDivisor* function, you will see it uses a **repeat** in place of the BASIC backward GOTO. The resultant program is easier to comprehend. It is, however, slightly less efficient in execution as the condition '*remainder* = 0' is tested twice. This is a common phenomenon; some loops are of the form

> *Start of loop*
>> *Action* 1
>> *Test the terminating condition and, if true, quit the loop*
>> *Action* 2
> *End of loop*

Such loops can be said to be executed 'N and a half times', for some N. You can sometimes conveniently turn these into ordinary loops by rephrasing the algorithm; otherwise they can only be expressed in Pascal by introducing small inefficiences like the one above, or, dare one say it, by the use of a **goto**. The inefficiences are a price most people are willing to pay. Some languages have a special statement which says 'quit the current loop'; this solves the problem.

Finally we notice that the BASIC INT function is not needed in our Pascal version, as we are working with integers anyway. Arguably, working with real numbers, as BASIC does, is an unnatural way of solving this problem.

Every call of a function f must execute at least one assignment statement of form

> $f := <expression>;$

Note that the use of a function name f on the left-hand side of an assignment is rather special; any other use of f would mean a call of f. The last such assignment to f defines the result to be returned. This is the purpose of the last line of *GreatestCommonDivisor*, which is

> $GreatestCommonDivisor := number2;$

There is no RETURN statement in Pascal. A function or a procedure automatically returns when it reaches its **end**, just as the main program automatically finishes when it reaches its **end**.

Procedures

A procedure is declared in exactly the same way as a function except that the heading line is written

> **procedure** *<name>* (*<list of parameters>*);

As with functions, the parenthesized list of parameters is omitted if there are no parameters. Here is a procedure to print the numbers 1 to *n*, one to a line.

```
procedure wastepaper(n: integer);
{ Prints the numbers 1 to n }
var
    index: integer;
begin
    for index := 1 to n do
        writeln(index);
end; { wastepaper }
```

A call of a procedure is written like a function call, except that a procedure call is a statement in itself, e.g.

wastepaper(6);
if $x > 0$ **then**
    wastepaper($q + 3$);

Given that procedures are similar to functions, much of what we say about one will also apply to the other. For the rest of this Chapter we shall therefore use the generic term *routine* to mean either a procedure or a function. It is a term borrowed from the language BCPL.

Built-in procedures

In the previous Chapter we introduced some of Pascal's built-in functions. In addition Pascal has a number of built-in procedures. Many of these are concerned with input/output, and, in fact, *writeln*, which we have already used in several examples, is one of them. You will come across several more built-in procedures – and functions – as you go through this book. Appendix A summarizes them all.

Some of Pascal's built-in routines illustrate a flagrant injustice. The systems programmers who define built-in routines have facilities available which are forbidden to you, the common user. In particular, built-in routines can have arguments that are optionally omitted, and, as shown by the input/output procedures, such as *writeln*, can have arbitrarily long lists of arguments of any type. You exploit these facilities when you call built-in routines, but they are denied to you when you define your own routines.

Local declarations

A routine can have declarations that are local to itself. Between the heading of the routine and its **begin** you can write a set of declarations of **labels, consts, types, vars** and indeed nested routine declarations. In the *GreatestCommonDivisor* function we have been modest with our local declarations. There is simply a single variable, called *remainder*. Further, the parameters *number1* and *number2* are treated as local declarations, so we have a total of three local variables. These local declarations are one of the most important features of Pascal. They mean that routines can be self-contained. This has three big advantages.

(1) There is no need to choose unique names for the local variables used in a routine. If any names you choose are already used outside the routine then your local usage overrides the outside usage. (BASIC has a hint of this with a declaration such as

   DEF FNA(X) = 3 − X / Y

Here the name X is local to the declaration of the function FNA.) The local usage can be completely different from the outside usage; the former, for example, could be a **type** and the latter a **var**.

(2) Mrs Buzz can set each worker to write a different routine without them interfering with one another.

(3) Routines are easier to debug and to maintain, because outside effects are reduced. A sound principle in program design is the idea of *information hiding*, due to Parnas (1972). Parnas's dictum is that details of how you represent and manipulate each set of objects should be confined to a few routines; this detailed information is hidden from the rest of the program, which treats these routines as black boxes.

Stepwise refinement

We have said that routines can themselves contain declarations of their own local routines. This helps program structuring, and in particular the method of structuring called *stepwise refinement*, which was introduced by Wirth himself (1971). In this method you first propound very powerful routines, and solve the problem using these. You next take each of your powerful routines and encode them using smaller routines. You carry this processs down until you have simple routines that you can code directly. An ideal adopted by many programmers is that the main program and the body of every routine should not exceed a page of text – fifty lines, say. The result is that the program, however big, is relatively easy to read. Do not worry, therefore, if you define a routine that is only called once; if this routine makes your program more readable, it earns its keep.

Local scope

In Pascal, all declarations have *scope*. The scope of a declaration is the routine in which the declaration occurs, together with any routines local to that routine, and any routines nested still deeper within these local routines, and so on. (Declarations in the main program have the whole program as their scope.) Outside its scope a declaration is unknown, and the same name can be used to mean something entirely different. There are two possible cases here: a name can be reused in disjoint non-overlapping scopes, or a name can be reused in a scope that lies within the scope of an earlier declaration. In the latter case, as we have said, the innermost declaration overrides the outer one(s). We illustrate these principles in the example below. The comments in the program explain the scope rules, and, for ease of reading, names are circled where they are declared.

```
program usa(input, output);
{ The names declared in the main program are all states of the USA }

var
    vermont: integer;
    ohio: real;

{ < < < < < < < < < < < < < < < < < < < < < < < < < < < < }

procedure oregon (lincoln: integer; eugene: real);
{ The local variables are names of towns and cities in Oregon }
const
    bend = 36;

type
    newport = (astoria, albany);

var
    salem: newport;
    foster: 1..bend; { a very small town }
```

```
{ < < < < < < < < < < < < < < < < < < < < < < < < < < < < < < < }
procedure (portland) ((fremont): newport);
{ The local variables are street names in Portland }

var
    (lombard): integer;
    (union): real;
    (vermont): 1..123; { no connection with the previous vermont }
    (foster): 1..bend; { no connection with the previous foster }

begin
    { Here all the above declarations are in scope, except for the outer
      vermont and foster, which have been overridden }
    {     .

          .
          }
          .
end; { portland }
{ This ends the scope of fremont, lombard, union,
  and the inner vermont and foster }
{ The previous vermont and foster are no longer overridden
  and come back into scope }
{ > > > > > > > > > > > > > > > > > > > > > > > > > > > > > > > }

begin { the body of oregon }
    {     .

          .
          }
          .
end; { oregon }
{ This ends the scope of lincoln, eugene, bend, astoria,
  albany, newport, salem, foster, portland }
{ > > > > > > > > > > > > > > > > > > > > > > > > > > > > > > > }

{ < < < < < < < < < < < < < < < < < < < < < < < < < < < < < < < }
procedure (maine) ((lincoln): real; (bangor): integer);
{ The local variables are names of towns and cities in Maine }
{ The above lincoln has no connection with the previous lincoln }

var
    (portland): 1..6; { no connection with the previous portland }
    (augusta): real;

begin
    { Here the declarations in scope are vermont, ohio, oregon,
      maine, lincoln, bangor, portland, augusta }
    {   .

        .
        }
end; { maine }
{ This ends the scope of lincoln, bangor, portland, augusta }
{ > > > > > > > > > > > > > > > > > > > > > > > > > > > > > > > }
```

```
begin { body of main program }
  { Here the declarations in scope are vermont, ohio, oregon, maine }
  {  ·
        ·
        ·  }
end.
```

Note especially the effect of the scope rules on the names of routines. You can only call a routine when its name is in scope. The name is in scope throughout the routine or program in which the name is declared. Thus *oregon* and *maine* can be called throughout the whole program, but the procedure *portland* can only be called from within *oregon*. There is a rider to this: a name can only be referenced after it has been declared; therefore *maine* cannot be called within *oregon*. If you have lots of routines that call one another, this can raise problems of ordering; we discuss these later.

Storage for variables

Coupled with local scope, there is a related mechanism called *local lifetime*. If a variable is local to a routine R, Pascal only allocates storage for the variable when R is called; on return from this call of R, Pascal releases the storage and the variable ceases to exist. While R is active it might call other routines, thus causing other variables to come and go, but this has no effect on the variables local to R. If R is called a second time, the same process is repeated; storage for its variables is reallocated and, on return from R, released again. Note that a variable dies when its storage is released. If the variable is reborn later as a result of another call, then the previous value is *not* carried over. Instead, every time a variable is born, it has an undefined value. (Pascal does not have a system, like certain non-standard BASICs, of initializing all variables to zero.)

Relating these rules to our example program, initially the variables *vermont* and *ohio* declared in the main program are allocated. These remain in existence throughout the execution of the program, and are therefore like variables in BASIC. Assume that the main program calls *maine*. At this point, variables *lincoln, bangor, portland* and *augusta* are born. (The first two of these are parameters and the other two are local variables, but all these quadruplets are born at the same time.) If *maine* subsequently calls *oregon*, then *lincoln* (no relation to the previous *lincoln*), *eugene, salem* and *foster* are born. If *oregon* in turn calls its own local procedure *portland*, then *fremont, lombard, union*, and new incarnations of *vermont* and *foster* are born. The variables that exist at this point are

$$
\left.\begin{array}{l} *vermont \\ ohio \end{array}\right\} \text{ belonging to the main program}
$$

$$
\left.\begin{array}{l} *lincoln \\ *bangor \\ *portland \\ *augusta \end{array}\right\} \text{ belonging to } maine
$$

$$
\left.\begin{array}{l} lincoln \\ eugene \\ salem \\ *foster \end{array}\right\} \text{ belonging to } oregon
$$

fremont
lombard
union } belonging to *portland*
vermont
foster

The variables marked with an asterisk are in hibernation. They cannot be referenced because they are not currently in scope. (Remember that variables can be out of scope for two separate reasons: they can be overridden, like *vermont* and *foster*, or they can belong to a separate non-overlapping procedure, like *maine*'s variables.) When hibernating variables come back into scope, as a result of a routine returning, they return to life unaffected by their sleep.

The variables in scope at any time are determined entirely by the layout of the program. On the other hand, the variables that are alive are determined by the dynamic behaviour of the program, and particularly by the routines that are active when a given routine is called. (In our example, *maine*'s variables happen to be alive when *oregon* is called.) It can, however, be guaranteed that all variables in scope are alive – otherwise programming would be a real nightmare.

After all the happy events come the funerals. When *portland* returns, its five local variables die. The original *vermont* and *foster*, previously overridden, come out of hibernation. When *oregon* returns, its four variables die, and the only variables left to attend the funeral are

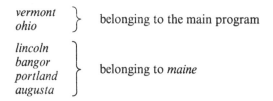

vermont
ohio } belonging to the main program

lincoln
bangor
portland } belonging to *maine*
augusta

All these are in scope. If *maine* calls *oregon* a second time then *lincoln*, *eugene*, *salem* and *foster* are reborn. (Quite likely they will occupy the same storage as they did previously, but this cannot be guaranteed and thus their initial values are undefined.) On return from *oregon* the new incarnations of these variables die again.

Finally *maine* will return, killing its local variables. The only two mourners will be the indestructible variables *vermont* and *ohio*.

Differences from permanent allocation

If you keep to the BASIC view of the world, i.e. that all variables except parameters have permanent storage reserved for them, your Pascal programs might still work, but you will miss two important points. One is concerned with recursion, discussed later, and the other is concerned with large arrays. You may have some large arrays that are only needed for a short time during program execution. If so, make each array local to a routine, and arrange your program so that you call the routine when you need the array and return when you have finished with it. (In some cases you may make several arrays local to a routine, but we assume a single one here.) The storage for the array is only reserved during the lifetime of the routine; for the rest of the time the storage is free, and can be used for arrays local to other routines. Thus the total size of your arrays may be bigger than the total storage available to you, but, by arranging non-overlapping scopes so that your arrays are not all in existence at the same time, you may still be able to run your program.

A language with the above mechanisms for local scope and for local lifetimes of variables is called a *block-structured language*. We mentioned this term earlier, without defining it; most, but certainly not all, of the widely-used modern languages are block-structured.

Adapting to block-structure

Many BASIC programmers do not reap the full rewards of Pascal because they are not accustomed to thinking in terms of block-structure. Do not fall into this trap. Emulate Mrs. Buzz and make the effort to divide your program into separate routines, none of them too long, and ensure that all your declarations are localized as much as they can be. Then, when you come to maintain your program, you will bless the magnificent programmer who wrote it.

To take a specific example of local scope, consider the *wastepaper* procedure defined earlier in this Chapter. The controlled variable of its **for** loop, *index*, has been made local to *wastepaper*. (It does not waste any storage to have lots of separate local variables that act as controlled variables to **for** loops; remember that local storage is only allocated when a routine is called.) Thus *wastepaper* is entirely self-contained.

If you are lucky, you have had the following experience. You have written a BASIC program of form

```
100  FOR K = 1 TO N
       .
       .
       .
200     GOSUB 3000
       .
       .
       .
300  NEXT K
```

and found it did not work. After hours of frustration you discovered that the subroutine at 3000 also used K in a FOR loop, with the result that the above call of 3000 upset the FOR loop that encloses it.

You may not have thought this lucky at the time, but now you have your reward. In Pascal you will always use a local variable to control all your **for** loops, and never get the same problem again. If, on the other hand, you have not learned your lesson, you will doubtless carry your BASIC habits over into Pascal, and take your punishment later.

Non-local variables

If you become convinced that local variables are extremely good value, you will doubtless, with the zeal of the convert, be tempted to over-use them. Thus we should warn you that there are a few places where local variables are inappropriate. One of these is illustrated by referring back to our *readcubed* function, which uses a variable, *readcount*, to count the numbers read. If you make *readcount* local to *readcubed* it dies every time you return from *readcubed*, thus losing its value. You must therefore declare *readcount* in the main program, or else in some routine which encloses *readcubed* and is active for the whole time the counting goes on. You also need to initialize *readcount* to zero before *readcubed* is first called.

The general principle is that you cannot make a variable local if you want its value carried over from one call to the next.

Recursion

A routine can call itself. This is termed *recursion* and is surprisingly useful. We shall provide examples later.

It is also possible to have a deeper kind of recursion called *mutual recursion*. Consider two procedures in a chess-playing program. One is called *BlacksBestMove* and the other *WhitesBestMove*. Each is passed a representation of the state of play as its argument. The strategy of *BlacksBestMove* is to postulate a possible move and then call *WhitesBestMove* to find out what the response would be. The procedure *WhitesBestMove* does the opposite. These procedures, which each call the other, are an example of mutual recursion. Mutual recursion can involve any number of procedures called to any depth. Clearly there must be some stopping condition to prevent the recursion getting ever deeper and deeper. Thus our chess-playing procedures might only look ahead to a depth of four moves, at which point the recursion stops.

In fact our *GreatestCommonDivisor* function can be encoded in a recursive way. This recursive version, which we have given the abbreviated name *gcd*, is declared as follows

```
function gcd(number1: posor0integer; number2: posor0integer): posor0integer;
{ Recursive equivalent of GreatestCommonDivisor function }
begin
    if number2 = 0 then
        gcd := number1
    else
        gcd := gcd (number2, number1 mod number2);
end; { gcd }
```

This version has the merit of working when either argument is zero, so we have used our type *posor0integer* rather than *positiveinteger*.

It is fair to warn you now that recursion is the kind of facility that is paradoxically described as 'Very easy once you know how'. The knowing how takes a bit of time for some, and if one glance at *gcd* makes you feel squeamish about the ruffled waters ahead, we suggest you travel by air, flying ahead until you reach the Section called 'Forward reference'.

The workings of *gcd* can be explained to the remaining fearless readers by considering the sample call

gcd (119, 98)

The basis of Euclid's algorithm is that the g.c.d. of 119 and 98 is the same as the g.c.d. of the two numbers 98 and 119 **mod** 98 (i.e. 21). If you keep applying this process you get ever smaller numbers, until one of the two numbers is zero; at this point the other one is the answer. Thus with our *gcd* function

$$gcd\,(119, 98) \tag{1}$$

calls

$$gcd\,(98, 21) \tag{2}$$

which in turn calls

$$gcd\,(21, 14) \tag{3}$$

which in turn calls

$$gcd\,(14, 7) \tag{4}$$

which in turn calls

$$gcd\,(7, 0) \tag{5}$$

The recursion now stops because *number2* $= 0$ is true. Thus, the deepest call of *gcd*, returns the result 7 to call (4), which itself returns the result 7 to call (3), and so on until the result of the outer call is returned as 7.

This is the magic of Euclid's algorithm. It worked perfectly in ancient Greece, and it still works perfectly today.

The recursive Pascal description of the algorithm is a natural one. In fact it reveals that the leaden hand of Frank Round had been at work on our original *GreatestCommonDivisor* algorithm. This BASIC-based original is harder to understand than the recursive description (once you are used to recursion).

Local variables and recursion

As a second example of recursion consider the function

```
function sumto0: integer;
var
    number: integer;
begin
    read(number);
    if number = 0 then
        sumto0 := 0
    else
        sumto0 := sumto0 + number;
end; { sumto0 }
```

Here *sumto0* is a function without arguments. It is called simply by writing its name. When you look at the line

$$sumto0 := sumto0 + number;$$

you might think this is simply incrementing the value of *sumto0*. However the syntax is rather deceptive. (Recall our earlier statement that a function name on the left of an assignment is something special.) The second *sumto0* is a (recursive) call of the function. Thus the line means 'the result of the function is obtained by calling *sumto0* recursively and adding the value of *number*'.

Before we explain what the function does, try to work it out for yourself. Consider the statement

> *writeln(sumto0);*

when the data supplied for the *read* consists of the numbers 13, 19 and 0.

The answer is that the function keeps reading data until a zero is supplied, and returns as its result the sum of the numbers passed over. It is exactly equivalent to

```
function sumto0: integer;
var
    number, sum: integer;
begin
    sum := 0;
    repeat
        read(number);
        sum := sum + number;
    until number = 0;
    sumto0 := sum;
end; { sumto0 }
```

It may surprise you that such a mundane operation can be expressed using recursion, and, moreover, that the recursive version is shorter. If you have just been battling away trying to work out what it does, you may not think, however, that the recursive version is more readable. In fact you may have failed to work it out at all.

In case this is so, we shall explain its workings. When first called, the function reads the value 13 and puts it in *number*. As *number* is not zero, the next action is the one following the **else**. This calls *sumto0* recursively. Now comes the real point that we want to make in this Section. At the recursive call, storage for *number* is allocated again. The previous allocation of *number* goes into hibernation – we cannot refer to it because the name *number* always refers to the latest allocation. This second call of *sumto0* sets its *number* to 19, and makes a further call of *sumto0* at a third level of recursion. This third call reads the value zero and puts it in its *number*. There are now three *number*s in existence. The one at the outer level has value 13, the one at the second level has value 19, and the current one has value 0. (The outer and second levels are both in hibernation.) The third level now finds that *number* = 0, and returns from the current call of *sumto0* giving 0 as the result of the function. At this point the third *number* is released and we go back to the second level. The second *number* becomes the current one, and, unaffected by the experience of hibernating for a while, still has the value 19. The statement

> *sumto0 := sumto0 + number;*

is resumed. Remember that the recursive call of *sumto0* caused it to be suspended. We now know the result of this call – it is 0. Thus this statement adds 0 to 19, and returns the result 19 as the value of the second call of *sumto0*. We are now back to a similar situation with the first call, and we add 19 to 13, getting 32 as the final result. Thus the effect of our original *writeln(sumto0)* is to print the value 32.

The whole workings depend on *number* being a local variable. If you declare it outside the function, storage will not be reallocated each time *sumto0* is called. Instead there will be only one copy of *number*. The result of *sumto0* would then always be 0, and it would not be a very useful function.

If our above explanation has been successful it will have convinced you that recursion and local variables go hand in hand to make a powerful combination. You may even believe Professor Primple's claim that recursion is the fundamental mechanism of programming. However, we fear that for many readers the reaction may be to regret they did not join the air travellers, who are just touching down now.

Forward reference

Big programs can contain hundreds of routines, and dozens of these might be declared at the same level of nesting. To make a program readable, there must be a consistent ordering, so that a reader stands a chance of finding a given declaration in the jungle. One possible ordering is alphabetical ordering of the routine names. However this leads to a problem we mentioned earlier: just like any other object, the name of a routine must be declared before it is used. What if procedure *aardvark* calls procedure *zebra*, or, worse still, *zebra* also calls *aardvark* in a mutually recursive manner? To surmount this problem, Pascal provides a mechanism for forward declarations. You can write, before *aardvark*, the declaration

> **procedure** *zebra(pig: real)*;
>   **forward**;

This counts as a declaration in the sense that *zebra* is now in scope and other procedures can use it. Later on, you must give the full declaration of *zebra*. When you do this, however, you must omit the parameter list because you have already mentioned this once and Pascal gets upset if you mention it twice. You thus might write

> **procedure** *zebra*; { *(pig: real)* }
> **var**
>   { ... }
> **begin**
>   { ... }
> **end**; { *zebra* }

It is a good idea to repeat the parameter list in a comment, as we have done above, so that the program is still readable in spite of Pascal's attempts to make it unreadable.

Similarly if *piggy* is a function to be declared forward, you can write

function *piggy*(*pig*: *real*): *integer*;
   forward;
{ .

      .
      . }

function *piggy*; { (*pig*: *real*): *integer* }
{ *The actual declaration follows* }

Changing the value of arguments

There is an important question that we have so far ignored: if the value of a parameter is changed, does the corresponding argument change too?

    Consider the following procedure

procedure *roundfigures*(*x*: *integer*);
{ *As we shall see, this procedure is useless* }
begin
    x := *x* − *x* **mod** 10; { *subtract from x the remainder from x/10* }
end; { *roundfigures* }

The aim of the above simple procedure is to convert its parameter *x* to the nearest multiple of 10 that is less than *x*. This is to help those laymen who do not really trust numbers, and feel happier if difficult numbers like 67 and 63 are expressed in 'round figures' as 60. Arguably 67 should be rounded to 70, but never mind.

    The procedure does not, however, achieve its purpose, because the normal rule in Pascal is that the parameter is a variable local to its procedure and any change in the parameter does not affect the corresponding argument. Thus in the call

    roundfigures(*temperature*);

the value of *temperature* is not changed. What happens is

(1) a local variable *x* is created and set to the current value of *temperature*, 67 say
(2) *x* is set to 60
(3) on return from *roundfigures*, *x* dies, thus causing the net effect of the call of *roundfigures* to be absolutely nothing

    In this particular example the desired aim can be achieved by writing *roundfigures* as a function rather than a procedure, but this will not always be the case.

    To achieve the desired aim in all cases, what is wanted is a mechanism to say that a parameter is to be treated exactly as a synonym of its corresponding argument, so that a change in one automatically causes a corresponding change in the other. Pascal has just such a facility; it consists simply of writing the word **var** in front of each parameter that is to be treated as a synonym. In the case of *roundfigures*, its heading should be written

    procedure *roundfigures*(**var** *x*: *integer*);

Synonym parameters are called *variable* parameters (or **var** parameters), and non-synonym parameters are called *value* parameters. The argument corresponding to a variable parameter must be identical in type to the parameter. This is the one place where compatible, but different, subrange types cannot be used. Moreover the argument must, quite naturally, be a variable. Thus the call

>   *roundfigures*(*temperature* + 6);

would be wrong. The argument can, however, be an array element. (We discuss arrays later; for the moment just think of *a*[*k*] in Pascal as A(K) in BASIC.) An example is

>   *roundfigures*(*a*[*k*]);

The effect here is that the value of k at the time of the call of *roundfigures* is calculated – we shall assume it has the value 6 – and the parameter is then treated as a synonym for array element $a[6]$.

Although the full discussion of arrays is still to come, it is worth mentioning now that whole arrays can be passed as arguments, and in this case the corresponding parameter is normally a variable parameter. This would apply, for example, to a procedure *invert*, which inverted a matrix supplied as argument.

Our procedures *roundfigures* and *invert* help to bring out a valuable programming technique. If a procedure has variable parameters, it can be self-contained yet can still communicate results back to the world outside it.

Routines as parameters

Very occasionally it is useful to have a routine name as a parameter to another routine. You may, for example, wish to call a procedure

>   *integrate*(*f*);

where *f* is a function name. Pascal has a mechanism for this, but the Pascal report differs from the Pascal standard, and, moreover, some compilers differ from both. Hence, if you really have a need for such a facility you must consult your local manual.

Building blocks

We shall close this Chapter by making a general point about programming style. This point is aimed at readers whose experience is only of the parameterless GOSUB and RETURN mechanisms of minimal BASIC, and who thus may not immediately appreciate the full benefits of their new-found freedom.

When you are faced with a difficult programming problem you probably solve it by a combination of 'top down' and 'bottom up' methods. The top down method is to start with the overall problem and continually divide it into sub-problems until these sub-problems are easy to program – the stepwise-refinement method epitomizes this. The bottom up method involves first sorting out the low-level details and encapsulating them in routines. These routines can then be used to attack problems at the next higher level of detail, and so on. The bottom up approach is only suitable when you know what direction you are going in.

Programming styles vary, but a typical approach is to first use the top down approach to reduce the problem to tractable parts, and then use the bottom up approach to program these parts.

Choosing the appropriate routines at each level of detail is one of the skills of programming. Often you will get them wrong first time, and your programs will be clumsy. After a while, your experience will tell you something is wrong. You will then respecify some of your routines; with luck, you will get them just right, and programming will become a dream. What you have done is something very important: you have built the right tools for the job.

Tools

The reason Man considers himself superior to other animals is because he uses tools. Tools have been the key to the advance of Man. Doubtless other animals, when they think about such things, take a contrary view, and consider themselves superior to Man. However, because few of these animals are likely to be our readers, we shall go along with Man's superiority here.

Tools are also immensely valuable in programming, and a good programmer is both a good tool-maker and a skilled user of tools. For a full discussion of this read Kernighan & Plauger (1981), a book that is a joy to read.

Creating a procedure or function is a way of building a tool. Once created, in order to perform a task in your program, a tool can be reused to help you whenever the same task arises elsewhere in your program. Moreover, if the tool is general enough, it can be put in a library (tool-chest), to be used by other programs.

Thus our advice to programmers who wish to evolve to become superior to their fellows is as follows: when you run into problems, build a self-contained tool to help. You can then reuse the tool to defeat the same problems whenever they arise in the future. Building tools is not easy, but, as we said in the previous Section, the more you practise, the better you become.

CHAPTER 6

More on
simple data types

So careful of the type she seems.

TENNYSON, *IN MEMORIAM*,
DESCRIBING HOW NATURE PRESERVES THE DIFFERENT
SPECIES

Geo.Boole 1815-64

Kinds of type

All the data types we have described so far have been *simple types*, which have a single value. In subsequent Chapters we shall consider other kinds of data type; in particular we shall cover arrays, which are collections of several objects. Given the term 'simple type', you might expect other types to be called 'complicated types', but no programming language ever admits anything to be complicated. Other types are felt to be simple too, though not quite so simple as simple types. It is a bit like washing powder: packets come in giant, jumbo and large sizes. There is no such thing as a small size.

Before we proceed to the not-quite-so-simple types, we shall, in this Chapter, complete our discussion of simple types by introducing two that have been so far omitted. These are *Boolean* and *char*. The former is named after George Boole (1815–1864), the logician, who has the unique distinction of having his name written down thousands of times a day by programmers all over the world. This is surely a better memorial than standing in a town square as a statue, with pigeons perched all over you. Thus give '*Boolean*' its capital letter when you write Pascal programs, even though your compiler will probably forgive you if you write '*boolean*'.

Boolean data

The Boolean data type contains only two values: *true* and *false*. The Boolean type effectively occurs in BASIC, though you may not have realized it. Relational expressions such as

$$X > Y$$

yield a Boolean result. In Pascal you can assign such a relational expression to a Boolean variable e.g.

```
var
    xpositive: Boolean;
    x: real;
begin
{   .
    .
    .
    }
    xpositive := x > 0;
```

Here the variable *xpositive* is set to *true* if *x* exceeds zero; otherwise it is set to *false*. As we said in Chapter 4, when you use an **if** statement (and similarly a **while** statement, etc.) in Pascal you are not confined to writing a relational expression, as we have done so far, but can write any Boolean expression. A Boolean expression is just like an arithmetic expression except that instead of manipulating numbers you manipulate the values *true* and *false*. The operands of a Boolean expression are relational expressions, Boolean variables or Boolean constants. The operators are **and**, **or** and **not**; these have the obvious meanings. The following are examples of the use of Boolean expressions

```
var
    xpositive, xorypositive, sunday, raining: Boolean;
    x, y, p, q: real;
begin
{   .

    .               }
    if xpositive then { ... };
    if not raining then { ...note that 'not' takes a single operand };
    while sunday and raining do { ... };
    xorypositive := xpositive or (y > 0);
    if (not raining or sunday) and (p > q) then { ... };
```

Note that in a sequence of statements such as

```
x := 15;
p := x + 3;
xpositive := x > 0;
x := x − 22;
```

the last statement, which changes x, does *not* change the value of *xpositive* (which remains true), for the same reason that it does not change the value of p.

Also note that if you find something like

if *xpositive* $=$ *true* **then** { ... };

in your program, then cut it out, because it was the sly Frank Round who put it there. The '$=$ *true*' is quite redundant.

The purpose of Boolean variables should be evident. They make programs easier to read and understand. Typical BASIC programs are obfuscated by numeric variables which take only the values 0 or 1, and are thus really Boolean. Your BASIC program may, for example, contain a variable K5 which is 1 if a certain initialization has been performed, and 0 otherwise. Similarly a variable M may be 1 if messages are to be printed, and 0 otherwise. Part of your BASIC program may read

```
      .
      .
      .
500  IF  K5 = 1  THEN  600
510  LET  K5 = 1
  .  ⎫
  .  ⎬  perform initialization
  .  ⎭
600 ...
      .
      .
      .
800  IF  K5 = 0  THEN  900
810  IF  M = 0  THEN  900
```

820 PRINT "INITIALIZATION DONE"
.
.
.
900 ...

You can write this in Pascal (using *initialized* for K5 and *sendmessages* for M) as

```
var
    initialized, sendmessages: Boolean;
begin
{   .
    .
    . }
    if not initialized then
    begin
        initialized := true;
        { ... perform initialization ... }
    end;
{   .
    .
    . }
    if initialized and sendmessages then
        writeln('initialization done');
```

Character data

A Pascal variable of type *char* can take as its value any single character. It is not therefore like a BASIC string variable, whose value consists of a sequence of several characters, but nevertheless it can be used as a fundamental building block from which strings can be made. Pascal strings are discussed in the next Chapter.

Every programming language that supports characters or strings has an associated *character set*. This specifies the set of allowable characters and an ordering of individual characters. In every character set the letters come in alphabetical order; thus 'B' invariably exceeds 'A'. Character sets may, however, differ as to whether, say, '+' exceeds 'A'; or even whether 'a' exceeds 'A'; you therefore court danger if you depend on a particular ordering. Early computer systems often had very limited character sets, based on card punching equipment, but a modern compiler and operating system should support enough characters to serve most of your needs. It is good if the ordering is based on an accepted standard such as the ASCII code.

A *char* constant, just like a character string, is enclosed in single quotes, e.g.

'a'

Thus when you transfer from BASIC to Pascal you must devalue all your quotes by half.

The following lines show some uses of a *char* variable.

```
var
    classcode: char;
begin
{   .
    .
    .   }
    classcode := 'a';
    if classcode = 'b' then {...};
    case classcode of { char and case often go together }
        'a': {...};
        'b': {...};
        'c', 'd': {...};
    end;
```

Operations on simple types

We have now seen the four simple types built into Pascal: *real*, *integer*, *Boolean* and *char*. These can be supplemented with user-defined types; in the rest of this Chapter we shall use as a sample user-defined type

> *animal* = (*mouse, dog, lion*); { *in ascending order of fierceness* }

In addition, a subrange of any simple type is also a simple type.

Associated with each data type are some operators that can be applied to objects of that type. These operators are

real	*, /, +, −
integer	*, **div, mod**, +, −
Boolean	**and, or, not**
char	(none)

The 'none' entry against *char* does not mean that *char* is useless. The relational operators (i.e. >, etc.), being polymorphic, can be applied to any simple types (and always give a Boolean result); moreover the assignment operator, e.g.

> *a* := *b*;

can be applied to any data type at all (except files, see Chapter 9). In general, where an operator has two operands (i.e. for any of the above operators except **not**), these two operands must be of the same data type, though, as we have said, *integers* and *reals* can be largely intermixed.

Pascal does not allow you to do eccentric things like **and**ing two reals or saying

> (1/2) * *true*

Pascal does not deal in half-truths.

You can easily construct Pascal expressions that involve a wealth of different operators, such as

> *a* := *b* > *c* **or not** *d* **and** *f*;

There is a set of precedence rules for determining the order in which operators are done. For example the rules say that the above assignment is equivalent to

$$a := b > (c \text{ or } ((\text{not } d) \text{ and } f));$$

which may surprise you. (**not** is done first, then **and**, then **or**; relational operators have lowest precedence.)

If you are uncertain of the relative precedence of two operators, do not, however, consult the Pascal report to find what the rules are. Instead put parentheses into your expression to make your intended meaning quite clear. As a result, readers of your program will not have to puzzle over what your program is trying to do.

Ordered sets of values

All simple types are represented by an ordered set of values. The following table shows the first, second and last members of the set of values associated with some simple data types.

Data type	First value	Second value	Last value
integer	−maxint	−maxint+1	maxint
Boolean	false	true	true
char	(defined by the character set)		
animal	mouse	dog	lion
1 .. 10	1	2	10

The data type *real* is exceptional. What is the next real after 2.0? The answer is that this is entirely dependent on the accuracy of the machine you are using. Unlike most of us, a Pascal compiler can forbid questions it cannot give a good answer to. As we shall see, it takes advantage of this.

Pascal's relational operators use these ordered sets of values. Pascal also supports several built-in functions, in addition to those with BASIC equivalents that we have mentioned already. Several of these relate to ordered sets of values. An important one is

$$ord(x)$$

which gives the 'ordinal number' of x in the set of values defined by the data type of x. The first value in the set has ordinal number 0, the second has ordinal number 1, and so on. Thus, as an example using our *animal* type, if the variable *beast* was set by the program

```
var
    beast: animal;
begin
{   .
    .
    .   }
    beast := dog;
```

then *ord(beast)* would be 1, because *dog* is the second value in the sequence of values in the data type *animal*.

If *x* is of type *char*, then *ord(x)* gives the position of *x* in the ordering defined by the character set. For doing the reverse translation to *ord*, there is a function *chr* which produces a *char* result; this function is such that

chr(ord(c)) is identical to c

for any character *c*. The function *chr* is therefore identical to the function CHR$ found in some BASICs, and, when applied to a character argument, Pascal's *ord* is like BASIC's CHR or ASC.

Finally, although you cannot add one or subtract one from, say, a *char* variable, you can achieve the equivalent effect with the functions *succ* and *pred*, which stand for successor and predecessor, respectively. The former is such that *succ(x)* is the successor of *x* in the data type defined by *x*. Thus *succ(2)* is 3, and, more to the point, *succ(mouse)* is *dog*, given the above definition of *animal*. The *pred* function does the opposite of *succ*.

If you ask for the *succ* or *pred* of a *real*, Pascal, as we have forewarned, will rule the question out of order.

The control of loops

We have been implicitly using *succ* and *pred* in some previous examples. This is because **for** ... **to** uses *succ*, and **for** ... **downto** uses *pred*, to alter the controlled variable. The pay-off from this is that the **for** statement is much more powerful and general than its use with integers shows. One can say

for *beast* : = *mouse* **to** *lion* **do**

in which case *beast* will successively take the values *mouse*, *dog*, and *lion*. Similarly

for *beast* : = *lion* **downto** *dog* **do**

will set *beast* successively to *lion* and *dog*. As a further example

```
var
    ch: char;
begin
{   .
    .
    .  }
    for ch := 'a' to 'z' do
        write(ch); { write(ch) is like PRINT C$; in BASIC }
    writeln; { this outputs a 'newline' character }
```

prints the line

abcdefghijklmnopqrstuvwxyz

provided that the letters '*a*' through to '*z*' are adjacent in the character set. In some character sets, notably EBCDIC, there are extra, rather peculiar, characters that come between some pairs of letters.

In most applications you should find plenty of scope for using more general **for** loops. Do not let Mr. 869704 rob you of this chance of creativity by confining your mind to numerical **fors**.

CHAPTER 7

Arrays
and strings

Harp not on that string.

RICHARD III'S ADVICE TO UNHAPPY PASCAL USERS

Basic concepts

Array references are basically similar in BASIC and Pascal except that Pascal encloses lists of subscripts in square brackets rather than round ones, e.g. BASIC's A(J,K) becomes Pascal's $a[j,k]$. Pascal not only allows arrays of one or two dimensions, like BASIC, but also permits arrays of three dimensions and more.

Pascal has no direct equivalent of the DIM statement; instead arrays are declared in the **var** section, just like any other variable. To achieve the equivalent of

DIM A(10), B(5,6)

you say

> **var**
> a: **array** $[0..10]$ **of** *real*;
> b: **array** $[0..5, 0..6]$ **of** *real*;

If you want any of your lower bounds to be 1 instead of 0, you can change the appropriate 0 to 1 in the above declaration. In fact you can, if you so wish, make a lower bound any other integer, such as 4 or even -4.

This use of integers as bounds, however, only gives a hint of the generality of Pascal. It may surprise you, but when you declare an array in Pascal you must give a data type to specify each pair of bounds. In our above examples we use types that are subranges of the integer type, for example $0..10$. The type could equally well have been a user-defined type, the type *char* or *Boolean*, or a subrange of any of these. (The only simple type not allowed is *real*.) Do not let Mr. 869704 deceive you into making all your array subscripts integers.

Associated with each array are at least two data types. These are the *component data type*, which is the data type of the array elements, and the *index data type*, which is the data type of the array index. (Pascal literature uses the word 'index' to mean 'subscript'.)

Hence in

c: **array** $['a'..'z']$ **of** *Boolean*;

the component data type is *Boolean* and the index data type is a subrange of *char*. The choice of index type is totally unrelated to the component type. If the array has several dimensions it can have several different index types, e.g.

ecount: **array** $['a'..'z', Boolean]$ **of** $0..1000$;

Given the above declaration, the elements of *ecount*, which are, of course, integers in the range 0 to 1000, can be accessed by subscripts such as

ecount $['p', false]$

Arrays such as this are not fanciful. Assume that you have the problem of counting, within a given text, for each letter '*a*' to '*z*'

(1) the number of words that begin with the given letter and end with the letter 'e'

(2) the number of words that begin with the given letter and do not end with the letter 'e'

Then the array *ecount* is just the data structure you need to do the counting. Taking the letter 'p' as an example, the element

    ecount['p', true]

measures the number of words that start with 'p' and end with 'e'. The corresponding *false* element counts the number that do not end with 'e'. The following program fragment shows how *ecount* might be updated.

```
var
    firstchar: char; {first character of current word}
    lastchar: char; {last character of current word}
    endswithe: Boolean;
    ecount: array['a'..'z', Boolean] of 0..1000;
begin
{   ·

    ·   }
{ Assume that at this point firstchar and lastchar have been set }
    endswithe := lastchar = 'e';
    ecount[firstchar, endswithe] := ecount[firstchar, endswithe] + 1;
{   ·

    ·   }
```

Think about this example, and also consider how you would program the same thing in BASIC. It should bring out several of the lessons that we have been trying to teach in this book.

Loops with arrays

Given that arrays in Pascal are normally accessed within loops, it is indeed fortunate that arrays and **for** statements fit so neatly together. Remember that, just as the index type of an array does not have to be an integer, neither does the controlled variable of a **for**. As an example of the use of non-integral data types, the following statement initializes all the elements of *ecount* to zero.

```
for row := 'a' to 'z' do
begin
    ecount[row, false] := 0;
    ecount[row, true] := 0;
end;
```

where *row* is declared as a variable of type *char*. In fact this initialization can be written using a nested loop, which covers the two values *false* and *true*. This is done as follows

```
for row := 'a' to 'z' do
    for column := false to true do
        ecount[row, column] := 0;
```

where *column* is a variable of type *Boolean*. You may recall that in Pascal every data type is an ordered set and that, in the case of *Boolean*, *false* is somewhat arbitrarily defined as less than *true*, as our table in Chapter 6 showed. (If you want an *aide-memoire*, remember that if a statement is 'less than true' it is false.)

An aside on error detection

As an exercise in the effects of errors, it is worth considering the effect of mistakenly writing the limits *false* and *true* in the wrong order, i.e.

```
for row := 'a' to 'z' do
    for column := true to false do
        ecount[row, column] := 0;
```

Null loops are quite acceptable in Pascal, as in BASIC. Therefore the effect of the above loop would not be to initialize *ecount*, but to do absolutely nothing, because the inner loop is null.

Fortunately most Pascal compilers check for *unassigned variables*, i.e. the use of variables that have not been given a value. Hence the first time you tried to use an element of *ecount* you would be given an error message. However this is usually an optional facility, and many bull-at-a-gate programmers switch the option off so that Perkins is kept away and their programs run more quickly. In this case, they would be duly rewarded: instead of giving errors their programs would proceed at great speed to produce quite random answers, because *ecount* would start with random values.

Declaring index types

In most cases the index type of an array will be a subrange type, such as

$$'a' .. 'z'$$
or $$1 .. 10$$

It is useful to follow our earlier advice by declaring such subrange types in the **type** section of the program, and giving them appropriate names, e.g.

```
type
    letters = 'a' .. 'z';
    lap = 1 .. 10; { assuming the array represents lap times for a 10 lap race }
```

The advantages of this are twofold. Firstly there may be several related arrays, all sharing the same index type. Declaring the type separately makes it easy to change. For instance you could change *lap* to 0 .. 12, and all the arrays using *lap* would change size correspondingly. Better still you could carry the naming a stage further and use a **const** called *numberoflaps* to represent our 10 or 12. This constant could be used in **for** loops that were applied to arrays with index type *lap*. Using these ideas we might have a program as follows

```
const
    numberoflaps = 10;
type
    laps = 1 .. numberoflaps;
    { We shall carry naming one stage further, and give a name to our array type }
    laptimes = array [laps] of real;
var
    harelaps: laptimes;           { lap times for the hare }
    tortoiselaps: laptimes;       { lap times for the tortoise }
    lapcount: laps;               { variable used as index to laptimes }
begin
    for lapcount := 1 to numberoflaps do { input the lap times }
        read(harelaps[lapcount], tortoiselaps[lapcount]);
{   .
    .
    .   }
```

The second advantage of giving the index type a name is that any variable used as an index to an array can be declared to be of the index type (see *lapcount* in the above example). This gives some added security. Nevertheless it brings us to make a comment, a comment that hurts us greatly to record. Although Perkins is an admirable fellow, and everything he does is intended to help, he really is a bit of a pain at times. One such time arises with a variable whose subrange type is just too small. We show an example of this below. The example also illustrates a valuable device in computing called a *stack*. If you have not come across stacks do not worry; you should still be able to understand the point of the example. The example is as follows

```
const
    stacksize = 100;
type
    stackrange = 1 .. stacksize;
var
    stack: array [stackrange] of integer;
    stacktop: stackrange;
begin
    stacktop := 1; { make the stack empty initially }
{   .
    .
    .   }
{ Now increment stacktop, checking for stack overflow }
    stacktop := stacktop + 1;
    if stacktop > stacksize then { ...give error message ... };
{   .
    .
    .   }
```

The point is that if *stacktop* becomes equal to *stacksize*, Perkins leaps to our aid when we try to increment *stacktop* by one and he stops the program then and there. He does not notice, of course, that the very next statement tests for that error. Thus we should have declared *stacktop* as

> *stacktop*: 1 .. *stacksize* + 1; { *But no!* }

Unfortunately this is not permitted. The Union of Pascal Constant Operatives, whose members work selflessly inside Pascal compilers trying to make sense of the miserable programs we feed them, requires subrange bounds to be constants. An expression such as 2 + 2 is too much and its members stop work straight away. To placate the Union, we would have to revise the start of our program to read

```
const
    stacksize = 100;
    overstacksize = 101; { the Union does not allow an expression here either }
{   .

    .
    .   }
var
    stacktop: 1 .. overstacksize;
```

Thus, to return to our original point, it is *sometimes* useful to declare variables used as array subscripts to be of the array's index type.

MAT statements

"I can see that this free choice of index types could possibly, in some limited circumstances, maybe sometimes help a tiny bit," said Bill, thus heaping greater praise on Pascal than ever before, "but how do you use them with MAT statements?"

As you doubtless know, several BASICs offer MAT statements, allowing operations such as

> MAT A = B + C

where A, B and C are arrays.

The answer to Bill's question – and he doubtless knew the answer when he asked – is that Pascal has no equivalent of MAT statements. Instead you have to write out all array operations in full, using **for** statements and the like.

The only exception is that you can assign one array to another, i.e. the equivalent of

> MAT A = B

in BASIC. This can be done only when the two arrays are identical in both component type and index type(s). It is achieved by an ordinary assignment statement, e.g.

> *a* := *b*;

Some Pascal compilers have the very strict rule (it is called 'name equivalence' in the next Chapter) that arrays are only identical if they are declared using an identical type identifier, as illustrated by the following example.

```
type
    rounds = array [1 .. 4] of integer; { scores in a golf tournament }
var
    a: rounds;
    b: rounds;
    c: array [1 .. 4] of integer;
begin
{   .
    .
    .  }
    a := b; { is legal because a and b have identical types }
{ .. but c := b; is illegal because b and c are not of identical type }
```

This serves to reinforce our advice to declare types and give them names. You then tell the compiler, and the reader of your program, which objects are the same and which objects differ.

Arrays of arrays

There are no restrictions on the component type of an array. Thus as well as arrays of reals, Booleans, etc., you can have arrays of arrays. You can, in fact, express any two-dimensional array as a one-dimensional array whose component type is itself a one-dimensional array. Thus an alternative to the declaration of *ecount* is

```
    newecount: array ['a' .. 'z'] of array [Boolean] of 0 .. 1000;
{ instead of
    ecount: array ['a' .. 'z', Boolean] of 0 .. 1000; }
```

Individual elements of *newecount* are then referenced by using two sets of brackets, e.g.

```
    newecount['p'] [false]
```

This in itself does not gain you anything – indeed you probably consider the notion somewhat contorted – but an array of arrays is useful in that you can assign sub-arrays (called *slices*) of the array to each other, or to other arrays of the same type. An example is

```
    newecount['c'] := newecount['k'];
```

If you picture an array in rows and columns, where the first subscript gives the row and the second the column, then the above statement assigns one row of *newecount* to another. In this case the rows only contain two elements so the assignment is equivalent, in the old notation, to

```
    ecount['c', false] := ecount['k', false];
    ecount['c', true] := ecount['k', true];
```

Our example of a two-dimensional array can be generalized to any number of dimensions. You can thus have arrays of arrays of arrays, or one-dimensional arrays of two-dimensional arrays, and so on.

An example

In order to give more of a flavour of the use of arrays in Pascal, we shall now show a somewhat longer example program. The example avoids fancy concepts like arrays of arrays and sticks to fundamentals.

The program is to do the following calculations. Some data consists of the number of calories consumed by a slimmer for each of the seven days of the week (starting on Monday) for five continuous weeks. Each week has a 'worst day', the day the slimmer consumed the most calories. The program keeps a count for Monday, Tuesday, etc., of how many times that day was the worst.

As well as news about their failings, slimmers also want encouragement. Although their calorie intake may have increased in a given week, they may have the slight compensation of consuming 20 fewer calories on one particular day, compared with the same day in the previous week. The program therefore tells them the greatest improvement (i.e. drop in calorie consumption) on a day of the current week compared with the corresponding day of the previous week. For the first week, however, it obviously cannot print this comparative figure. Here is the program.

```
program slimmer(input, output);
type
    day = (monday, tuesday, wednesday, thursday, friday, saturday, sunday);
    calorieintake = 0 .. 9999; { day's calorie intake }
    caloriecounts = array [day] of calorieintake;
var
    calories: caloriecounts;      { current week's calorie counts }
    lastcalories: caloriecounts; { previous week's calorie counts }
    worstcount: array [day] of integer;
    worstday: day;
    today: day;
    improvement: integer;
    bestimprovement: integer;
    week: integer;
    firstweek: Boolean;
begin

{ **** 1: initialization **** }

    firstweek := true;
    for today := monday to sunday do { initialize worst day counts }
        worstcount[today] := 0;

{ **** 2: main loop to perform weekly calculations **** }

for week := 1 to 5 do
```

```
begin
    for today := monday to sunday do { read the data }
        read(calories[today]);
    worstday := monday; { initial setting }
    if not firstweek then
        bestimprovement := lastcalories[monday] – calories[monday];
    for today := tuesday to sunday do
    begin { reset worstday and/or bestimprovement as necessary }
        if calories[today] > calories[worstday] then
            worstday := today;
        if not firstweek then
        begin { compare with last week }
            improvement := lastcalories[today] – calories[today];
            if improvement > bestimprovement then
                bestimprovement := improvement;
        end;
    end; { for loop }
    { At the end of the week:
        print bestimprovement and update counts of worst day }
    if firstweek then
        firstweek := false
    else
        writeln('Best improvement in week', week, 'was', bestimprovement);
    worstcount[worstday] := worstcount[worstday] + 1;
    lastcalories := calories; { an array assignment }
end; { weekly loop }

{ **** 3: final printing **** }

    writeln;
    writeln('Number of times each day was the worst is as follows');
    for today := monday to sunday do
        writeln(worstcount[today]);
end.
```

Given the data

```
1596 1789 1500 2198 2709 1608 1763
1754 3408 2316 1908 1965 2076 1543
2409  987 1543 1765 1289 2341 1913
1720 1523 1482 1723 2178 1523 1478
3001  981 1234 2900 2709 2510 2301
```

the *slimmer* program would produce the output

Best improvement in week	2 was	744
Best improvement in week	3 was	2421
Best improvement in week	4 was	818
Best improvement in week	5 was	542

Number of times each day was the worst is as follows

2
1
0
0
2
0
0

You could improve upon the logic of this program. As it stands, if two days are equally bad, the program only counts the earlier one, thus giving a bias to the results. You could also improve its printing, as we shall explain at the end of Chapter 9.

Bad news

If you are a reader with a wide knowledge of programming languages, we have some bad news for you. If, on the other hand, your travels are limited to simple BASICs, keep smiling for a while – the initial impact of the tragedy will seem to be in a distant land.

The news is that Pascal provides no mechanisms for arrays of variable size. For BASIC users, it is equivalent to saying there is no

DIM X(N)

where N is a variable; this should come as no surprise. In many other languages, however, variable-sized arrays are allowed, and their absence from Pascal is a disappointment to some (even if they have been forewarned by the previous discussion of Union rules).

Given this news, a further question arises. Can you write a procedure whose parameter is an array of variable size? It would certainly be valuable to write a procedure to, say, invert a matrix of any size. A procedure that can invert only 5 × 5 matrices is much less useful.

The answer to the question is unfortunately not definitive. The so-called 'Level 1' of the Pascal standard (though not the Pascal report) allows array parameters to be of variable size, but it takes several years for compilers in the field to be modified to a new standard. Worse still, there are many compilers in existence which allow array parameters of variable size, but do this in a different way from the standard. Thus all we can offer is the somewhat vacuous advice to consult your local Pascal manual, and to beware of portability problems.

A further restriction in Pascal is that a function must return a simple type as its value. It cannot therefore return an array, though, as the next Section will show, it can assign a value to an array passed as an argument.

An example of an array parameter

The following example shows the use of an array parameter. The array is of fixed size, being of ten elements.

```
type
    vector10 = array [1 .. 10] of integer;
var
    x: vector10;
    y: vector10;

procedure settozero(var a: vector10);
var
    k: integer;
begin
    for k := 1 to 10 do
        a[k] := 0;
end; { settozero }

begin
    settozero(x); { sample call of the procedure }
    settozero(y); { another sample call }
{    .
     .
     .  }
```

This example serves to illustrate a further point. An important consequence of the rule for **var** parameters is that if you want to change any or all of the elements of the array passed as argument, then you must not forget the **var**. If we had forgotten it for the parameter *a* to our procedure *settozero*, the effect would be as follows

- the argument array, *x* say, would be copied to a local array called *a*

- *a* would be set to zero

- on return from *settozero*, *a* would disappear

- the original array *x* would be unchanged; thus the net effect of the procedure call would have been to do absolutely nothing. (This example in fact mirrors our *roundfigures* example in Chapter 5.)

Packed arrays

Let us assume that you possess two alternative storage cabinets for your clothes, each containing a number of drawers of a standard size. One cabinet has four of these standard-sized drawers, and the other has a single standard-sized drawer.

Being modest in your sartorial needs, you can just pack all your clothes into the single-drawer cabinet. The clothes are quite hard to extract, but they are nice and compact and easy to move about as a whole. The alternative is to use the four-drawer cabinet, putting socks in the first drawer, shirts or blouses in the second and so on. The clothes will then be easier to extract, but they will be less compact – three-quarters of each drawer will be empty. They will also be harder to move about as a whole.

Exactly similar considerations apply to packing data inside the computer. When you declare an array or record (see later) in Pascal you can give it the attribute **packed**. This tells the compiler that you are more interested in compactness than speed of access to individual elements. The compiler may or may not take any notice of your advice; it depends greatly on what data packing facilities are available on your computer. On some machines **packed** can certainly make the difference between the data fitting inside the machine and the data being too big.

The only language facility you lose with packing is that an individual element of a packed array cannot be used as a **var** parameter to a procedure or function call. It is quite permissible to pass a whole packed array, provided that both the argument and the parameter are declared as **packed**. We could, therefore, have changed the above *settozero* example by declaring *vector10* as

vector10 = **packed array** [1 .. 10] **of** *integer*;

and the program would remain valid.

Three possible guidelines for using packing are

- you gain most by packing arrays of small objects, such as *char* data, Boolean data, or small subranges of integers. We shall see shortly that packed characters are of particular significance in Pascal

- if you frequently access the array as a whole (e.g. by assigning it to another array or passing it as a non-**var** parameter) then this favours packing, as compact data is easier to move about

- if you frequently access individual elements of the array, this makes packing less attractive

A good and painless way of assessing the value of packing on your machine is to sneak a few **packed**s into a friend's program. If, on the next day, he proudly tells you how much he has improved his program's performance, you will know that packing is good and can try using it selectively in your own program.

Pascal provides built-in procedures, called *pack* and *unpack*, for copying an unpacked array into a packed one, and vice-versa (see Appendix A).

Strings in BASIC

We shall now introduce the topic of string data. Implementations of BASIC differ greatly in the facilities they offer for manipulating strings. However they have one thing in common: they are all better than Pascal. It comes as something of a shock that the apparently simple string manipulation facilities typical of BASIC not only outdo Pascal, but even outdo most of the bright new up-to-the-minute languages studied by Professor Primple and his colleagues.

Most BASICs support strings of dynamic length, i.e. whose length may vary from nothing to the size of the string. Thus you can say

LET S$ = "GETS "
LET S$ = S$ & "LONGER"

The '&' operator concatenates the previous value of S$ with LONGER, thus setting S$ to GETS LONGER. The result is that the length of S$ has increased. Many BASICs, even on the feeblest micros, allow strings to vary in length from zero to 255 characters. Perhaps you never realized this was a luxury feature.

Strings in Pascal

A string variable in Pascal is represented as a packed array of *char*. (Some BASICs adopt a similar approach, and allow string variables to be accessed as if they were arrays of single characters.) The array must have 1 as its lower bound. The Pascal equivalent of the BASIC

```
LET R$ = "yes"
LET N$ = "Peter"
```

is

```
var
    reply: packed array [1 .. 3] of char;
    name: packed array [1 .. 5] of char;
begin
    reply := 'yes';
    name := 'Peter';
```

By declaring string variables in this way, you get all the facilities normally associated with arrays in Pascal. You can thus say

```
reply[j] := name[3];
```

to assign the third character of *name* to the *j*th character of *reply*. Moreover you get three extra facilities unique to strings

(1) you can assign a string constant to a string variable; the last two lines of the introductory example are instances of this
(2) you can apply relational operators to string variables and/or constants
(3) you can output string variables or constants (but not, as we shall see in Chapter 9, input them, except one character at a time)

An example illustrating (2) and (3) is

```
if name < > 'Bruce' then
    writeln(name, ' is not an Australian');
```

String variables in Pascal are of static size, i.e. their length is always the size of the array in which they are stored. Thus *reply* must always have a value of exactly three characters, and *name* must have a value of exactly five characters. You cannot, therefore, say

```
name := reply;
```

because you would be trying to give *name* a three-character value. Similarly, it turns out that both Bill Mudd and Professor Primple are correct when they pronounce from their different viewpoints that you cannot compare BASIC with Pascal. The relational expression

   'BASIC' > 'Pascal'

is likely to give you an error, as the two strings are of different length. If you knock the 'l' out of Pascal, you could try

   'BASIC' > 'Pasca'

and, to Bill's chagrin, the result would be *false* because the ' > ' operator uses the natural dictionary ordering. Likewise if you added a space to the end of BASIC. Incidentally the relation

   'BASIC ' > 'pascal'

would give undefined results because, as we have said, character sets may vary as to whether the upper case letters come before the lower case ones.

   As you probably have now realized, the Union of Pascal String Processors is even stronger than the Union of Pascal Constant Operatives. It is so strong, in fact, that its members hardly do any work at all. Certainly you could not get them to pad a string variable with spaces to make up the required length. You might just be able to persuade them to pad a string constant with the appropriate number of spaces. For example they might accept

   reply : = *'no'*;

as a substitute for

   reply : = *'no '*;

Consult your local Pascal manual for details, as some compilers do offer non-Union extensions.

   It will, however, have to be a much extended compiler to offer facilities such as concatenation, or operators that extract substrings of strings, like LEFT$, RIGHT$ and SEG$ found in some BASICs. If present, such facilities make for non-portable programs, unless the extended Pascal is so good that it becomes a *de facto* standard – which does sometimes happen. Most Pascals do not allow you even to define a function that returns a string result, because functions cannot return an array as their result.

   If you previously regarded the Pascal restrictions on arrays as a tragedy in a distant land, you may, having seen the impact on strings, feel that the tragedy is closer to home.

   Professor Primple has even found some problems with Pascal's restrictions on strings.

   "My program to analyse English sentences works well," he said, echoing a familiar theme, "but there is a small restriction that all sentences must contain ten words and each word must be of five letters."

   Bill Mudd's comments about this aspect of Pascal cannot be packed into a fixed-length string.

Surmounting the restrictions

If you are now in despair, you will be somewhat heartened to hear that you can get round the Union intransigence by building your own dynamic-length strings. Thus it would actually have been possible for Professor Primple to avoid the small restrictions in his program.

Dynamic-length strings can be achieved, for example, by associating two variables with each of your strings: one an integer giving its current length and the other a Pascal string variable whose length is the maximum length of your string. You can then write procedures to manipulate these strings of yours. These procedures only process characters up to the current length; characters beyond, though present, are ignored. (If you want to get a flavour of this technique, look ahead to page 118.) Each string passed to these procedures is represented as a pair of arguments, giving the two variables associated with the string. You might have a procedure

assign(*length*1, *string*1, *length*2, *string*2);

which assigns one string to another. This procedure could be used instead of Pascal's built-in facilities for string assignment, and you could write similar procedures to take over the rest of Pascal's facilities.

The overall result of your efforts would not be pretty, and string constants would remain a tedious problem, but you could at least distance yourself from Union restrictions. The use of records, described in the next Chapter, enables you to represent each of your strings as a single record, rather than the pair of quantities described above; this helps with program conciseness.

There are, as an alternative, some proposals in the literature concerning strings in Pascal; see Bishop (1979) and Sale (1979). These represent strings as files, and you have to do odd things such as rewinding strings before you reuse them. Nevertheless if you are desperate you cannot afford to be too fussy about odd quirks.

CHAPTER 8

Records

My record speaks for itself.

POPULAR CLAIM

Declaring a record

People in commercial computing have been using the concept of a *record* since the late fifties. It has taken a while for the rest to catch up with them, and Pascal is one of the first languages to make records popular in wider fields.

A record is used to construct a new data type that is made up of a collection of other data types (which may be, and usually are, different from one another).

The following example shows how records are declared and used.

```
type
    applicant =
        record
            weight: 1 .. 30; { weight in stones }
            age: 0 .. 150;
            lovesPascal: Boolean { Primple says omit this semicolon } ;
        end;
var
    Primple: applicant;
    Mudd: applicant;
    currentapplicant: applicant;
```

Here the record *applicant* consists of three *field*s: the age and weight of the applicant, and the Boolean *lovesPascal*, which is *true* if the applicant loves Pascal. (For the benefit of those brought up in uncivilized countries which do not use such units as chains, rods, poles and perches, and probably do not play cricket either, our unit of weight is a 'stone'. A stone is fourteen pounds. A pound is, of course, the weight of one-tenth of an imperial gallon of water. A gallon is .... .)

The only operation you can perform on a variable that is a record is to assign it to another variable, which has been declared as an identical record. Thus you can say

```
currentapplicant := Primple;
```

or, to stretch the imagination,

```
Primple := Mudd;
```

There are no constants of type record, any more than there are array constants (apart from strings).

Structured types

Records and arrays in Pascal are both called *structured type*s, and share many qualities. We have just seen that you cannot do much with records *as a whole*, just as you cannot with arrays. Instead you perform most operations on individual elements. The elements of arrays are accessed via subscripts; the fields of records, on the other hand, are accessed via *field identifier*s. The field identifiers are the names that are written before the components of the record, i.e. *weight, age* and *lovesPascal* in our example. You cannot, of course, have two fields with the same name within one record, such as two *age*s. You can, however, use the same field identifier within two separate records. Thus other records besides *applicant*s can have an *age*.

When you wish to access a field of a record, you write a dot after the name of the record variable, and then append the field identifier, e.g.

> *Primple.age* := 45;
> *Mudd.lovesPascal* := *false*;
> **if** *birthday* **then**
>   *Primple.age* := *Primple.age* + 1;

As further examples, the assignment statement

> *currentapplicant* := *Mudd*;

is exactly equivalent to

> *currentapplicant.weight* := *Mudd.weight*;
> *currentapplicant.age* := *Mudd.age*;
> *currentapplicant.lovesPascal* := *Mudd.lovesPascal*;

It can be seen that the notation for accessing fields of records is slightly different from the notation for accessing array elements, e.g.

> *recordvar.field*   as against   *arrayvar[subscript]*

This difference is reasonable; it makes it clear to a reader whether a record or an array is being accessed – there is no need to consult the declaration.

Fields of records, just like array elements, can be used as ordinary variables. Again, like arrays, records can be **packed**, with similar potential advantages.

Data structuring

You may have noticed a similarity between the **begin** and **end** used to group statements together, and the **record** and **end** used to group data together. This gives a clue to the fundamental usage of records: to help Mrs Buzz give a structure to data, just as **begin** and **end**, together with other constructs, help her give a structure to the statements within a program. Each is equally important. The title of Wirth's book *Algorithms + data structures = programs* (1976) says it all.

Just as you can nest **begin**s and **end**s, you can nest records. To show this, we shall change our *applicant* record to contain a date of birth instead of an age field. Some prospective employers ask for both age and date of birth on their application form, and weed out all those whose age does not square with their date of birth; computer science graduates are said to fail this test more than most. As we do not want to be hard on computer scientists, we shall dispense with the redundant *age* field. The date of birth will itself be a record, which consists of a day, a month and a year. Thus we can declare our revised record as

```
type
    applicanta =
        record
            weight: 1 .. 30;
            birthdate:
                record
                    day: 1 .. 31;
                    month: (Jan, Feb, Mar, Apr, May, Jun, Jul, Aug, Sep, Oct,
                                                                    Nov, Dec);
                    year: 1850 .. 2000;
                end;
            lovesPascal: Boolean;
        end;
```

We could equally well have written the above as

```
type
    date =
        record
            day: 1 .. 31;
            month: (Jan, Feb, Mar, Apr, May, Jun, Jul, Aug, Sep, Oct, Nov,
                                                                    Dec);
            year: 1850 .. 2000;
        end;
    applicantb =
        record
            weight: 1 .. 30;
            birthdate: date;
            lovesPascal: Boolean;
        end;
```

The advantage of nested records should be obvious, as nested records are analogous to other nested structures. The advantage is that you can treat as a unit a subrecord, like *birthdate*, which lies within a larger record.

To access a field that is nested *n* levels deep in a record, you should specify all the *n* field identifiers that are needed to 'find' the field, starting at the outermost record, e.g.

Primple.birthdate.month := *Feb*;

The above example applies irrespective of whether the record was declared as in *applicanta* or as in *applicantb*. Field identifiers in inner records must not be the same as in outer ones, but in spite of this you must still write all *n* identifiers.

Facilities for nesting

Several years ago an emotive advertising slogan, encouraging British people to emigrate to Australia, said 'In Australia you can'. (The advertisement did not record the matching sayings within Australia, describing what Britishers can do.)

If you want to adopt Bill's style of programming the corresponding slogan for Pascal might be: 'In Pascal, you can't'. We discussed, in Chapter 2, the discipline imposed by Pascal.

There is, however, one area where the slogan is definitely 'In Pascal, you can'. This is the area of nesting. Thus you can almost invariably carry nesting as deeply as you reasonably want to, and you can nest anything within anything else. If you ask whether a facility x is allowed within a record, the answer will therefore be 'yes'. Hence you can have arrays of records, or records containing arrays, or you can combine the two as in

```
array26 = array [2 .. 6] of real;
deepnest = array [1 .. 5] of
    record
        a: array26;
        b: array [3 .. 7] of
            record
                c: real;
                d: array ['a' .. 'e'] of Boolean;
            end;
        z: integer;
    end;
```

Such a structure could be accessed as follows

```
var
    x: deepnest;
    yarray: array26;
begin
{   .
    .
    .   }
x[1].b[3].d['c'] := true;
yarray := x[2].a; { a reference to a whole array, within a record }
```

An alternative view

"All this stuff about structuring is all very well," said Bill, "but what use are these records? All you can do is assign them to other records. It seems to be yet another instance of redundant rubbish being added to programs."

Bill is writing a book of his own. It is called *BASIC from Pascal*. He expects it to be the greatest best seller of all time, and was kind enough to show us an early draft. The first page contains the stirring advice:

"Are you having trouble remembering all the data types in Pascal? Do you have difficulty deciding which to use? Are you worried about academic pussyfoots reading your declarations?"

"Forget the lot. The world consists solely of numbers and strings, plus arrays of either. You can always reduce any real problem to these data types, provided you chop the problem about enough. Don't worry about the pussyfoots either, the chances are that no one but you will be able to figure out what your variables are doing – so no one will be able to criticize".

An example

Whatever the merits of Bill's arguments, he does rather underestimate the useful-ness of records 'that can only be assigned to other records'. This is because one example of assignment is passing as an argument. You can therefore write procedures and functions to manipulate the records you have defined.

Let us choose as example the record

```
complex =
    record
        realpart: real;
        imaginary: real;
    end;
```

This describes a *complex number*, which is a concept much used in mathematics and engineering, and hence in computer programs. Complex numbers were, by their very name, invented a long time ago. Nowadays, as we have already obser-ved, the public relations men would have dubbed them 'simple numbers' or the like, to distinguish them from ordinary 'very simple' numbers.

For those who have not come across complex numbers, or who have happily forgotten about them, we should explain that a complex number is a pair of numbers, one of which is called the *real* part and the other the *imaginary* part.

There is a set of rules for defining arithmetic operations on complex num-bers. Two rules are shown below: the notation (x, y) means a complex number with real part x and imaginary part y.

Addition: $(a,b) + (c,d) = (a+c, b+d)$
Multiplication: $(a,b) * (c,d) = (ac-bd, bc+ad)$

Given these rules you might think it would be easy to write a set of Pascal functions to perform complex arithmetic. However this is not possible because the result of a Pascal function must be a simple data type, whereas our needs call for functions that return complex numbers (i.e. records) as their result. Hence we have to formulate the operations as procedures, rather than as functions.

Our procedure to perform complex addition is

```
procedure addcomplex (var x: complex; y, z: complex);
{ This sets x := y + z; where x, y and z are complex numbers }
begin
    x.realpart := y.realpart + z.realpart;
    x.imaginary := y.imaginary + z.imaginary;
end; { addcomplex }
```

A similar procedure to do multiplication is

```
procedure multiplycomplex (var x: complex; y, z: complex);
{ This sets x := y * z; where x, y and z are complex numbers }
begin
    x.realpart := y.realpart * z.realpart – y.imaginary * z.imaginary;
    x.imaginary := y.imaginary * z.realpart + y.realpart * z.imaginary;
end; { multiplycomplex }
```

Given these procedures a complex operation such as

$$c1 := c2 + c3 * c4;$$

can be programmed as

multiplycomplex(temp, c3, c4);
addcomplex(c1, c2, temp);

where *temp* is a variable of type *complex*.

These procedures are reminiscent of the MAT routines found in some BASICs. The only difference is that here we have defined our own operations – we do not have to rely on them being built into the language. (We could have defined our own exact equivalents of the MAT statements if Pascal allowed arrays of variable size as arguments.)

As an alternative way of writing our complex arithmetic procedures, we could, in the main program, have defined a complex variable called *accumulator*, and revised our procedures to leave the result of their operation in this accumulator. The procedures would then not need the argument x, and the style of programming would become similar to that of a typical assembly language (the low-level language for a particular machine), e.g.

multiplycomplex(c3, c4);
addcomplex(c2, accumulator); { *result is now in the accumulator* }

Abstractions

Our example of complex numbers shows a highly productive style of programming. What we do is to define our own data type, *complex*, plus a set of procedures to work on that data type. The final achievement is almost as good as having *complex* built into Pascal in the first place; the only tarnish is that the syntax for using our procedures is rather clumsy, though not intolerably so.

What we have created is a *data abstraction*. This is an abstraction away from Pascal's built-in data types, and towards the problem being solved. Pascal, though far from being the perfect tool, is an aid in achieving this. Notice how the detail of how to do complex arithmetic is banished into the bodies of our procedures. The main program is therefore free of this low-level detail, and easier to understand as a result. This is an example of information hiding.

Professor Primple, a name greatly associated with abstraction, believes abstraction to be the most important programming aid.

Test the validity of his view by doing some abstractions of your own. Whenever you have one or more related variables in a program (such as a stack and the top-of-stack pointer), group these variables together as a record. Then define some procedures and, if appropriate, functions to manipulate the records. Does the programming become easier? More importantly, is your program easier to read? Can the reader, for example, easily separate the overall concepts from the details, and look at either in isolation?

The *with* statement

Let us return to our *applicants*, who have been kept waiting rather too long.

Our task is to write a function *evaluate*, which evaluates an *applicant* for a particular programming job. The job specification calls for someone about 35 years old who loves Pascal. The appointee has to share a terminal, so the applicant needs to be heavy enough to push someone else off. The function *evaluate* returns a 'score' that rates the suitability of the applicant; the higher the score the better. The function is as follows

```
function evaluate (person: applicant): integer;
{ Evaluates suitability of applicant for a job }
var
    score: integer;
begin
    score := person.weight; { one point for each stone of weight }
    if person.lovesPascal then
        score := score + 50;
    if (person.age > 25) and (person.age < 45) then
        score := score + 20;
    evaluate := score;
end;   { evaluate }
```

(Perkins says, quite rightly, that this function would be improved by defining a subrange type and using it in place of each occurrence of *integer*.)

The function can be called by code such as

```
if evaluate(Primple) > evaluate(Mudd) then
    write('Primple')
else
    write('Mudd');
writeln(' gets the job');
```

When encoding the *evaluate* function, it was rather tedious writing 'person.' numerous times. To save this tedium Pascal provides a shorthand notation whereby you can say 'Within this context, every field refers to record variable *x*'. This is done by the **with** statement, which has a syntax (though not a meaning) akin to a **while** statement. Using **with**, the executable part of *evaluate* can be rewritten as

```
begin
    with person do
    begin
        score := weight; { one point for each stone of weight }
        if lovesPascal then
            score := score + 50;
        if (age > 25) and (age < 45) then
            score := score + 20;
    end;   { scope of with }
    evaluate := score;
end;   { evaluate }
```

Likewise the executable part of *addcomplex* can be written

```
begin
    with x do
    begin
        realpart := y.realpart + z.realpart;
        imaginary := y.imaginary + z.imaginary;
    end;
end; { addcomplex }
```

though here the gain from using **with** is at best marginal. The example shows, however, that inside **with** you can refer to records that are not the subject of the **with**.

There are more elaborate forms of **with** that you can try when you have got used to the simple case, and you can, of course, nest **with**s. Consult the Pascal report for details. Bear in mind, though, that the idea of a **with** is to make your program easier to write and to read, so a complicated one destroys its very purpose.

Remember two points about **with**. Firstly you can use it where you like; its use is not confined to procedures. Secondly it is simply a shorthand notation; it does not imply looping or the like.

There is, in fact, no facility for looping associated with a record. This is in contrast to an array, where a **for** statement can be used to loop through the elements. If you think about it, you will realize that performing the same operation on each field of a record is rarely a sensible thing to do, because the fields are generally of different data types.

Given the lack of a concept of looping, the order in which you write the fields of a record is entirely your choice (except for 'variant' fields described in the next Section). We could, for example, interchange the order of *age* and *weight* without affecting our programs at all.

Variant records

One of the problems of programming in the real world is that objects are not uniform. Thus if a record in a program describes a person, then a married person has a spouse whereas a single person does not. If the person works in a company and is salaried, then the data required is different to that for a wage earner; if the person is an alien his tax data will be different.

To allow for this, Pascal permits a record to contain one *variant field*, which must come at the end of the record. The variant field can take on different forms, depending on some specified criterion. Be warned, however: even the smoothest public relations man would find it hard to convince you that the initial impression of this feature is other than very complicated. Therefore grit your teeth for what is to come.

We shall use as an example a stock of spare parts in a storeroom. These parts fit into two categories: some of them possess an integer called the 'part number', and are represented by this part number, together with a 'class code', giving the strength of the part as *robust*, *normal* or *delicate*; the parts that do not have a part number are represented by a string of ten characters that acts as the 'part name'.

Associated with a variant record is a *discriminator* field to say which of the possibilities applies. In our case the discriminator can be a *Boolean*, because there are only two possibilities. We have called it *hasnumber*. The declaration of the record is

```
type
    strength = (robust, normal, delicate);
    nameofpart = packed array [1 .. 10] of char;
    part =
        record
            cost: integer;
            {   .

                .
                .  }
            case hasnumber: Boolean of
                true: (
                    partnumber: integer;
                    classcode: strength
                        );
                false: (
                    partname: nameofpart
                        );
        end;
```

This somewhat complicated syntax says what we have tried to explain in words above. In detail, it says that the last field has several possible **cases** – arguably Pascal's use of the word **case** here is a mistake as the syntax is not quite the same as the **case** statement described in Chapter 4. If you wish, mentally substitute **variant** for **case** in this Chapter. (However your unforgiving compiler will still expect the word **case**.) The word **case** is followed by a declaration of the discriminator field that will be used to select the variant. Within the body of the **case**, each possible value of the discriminator is followed by a list (possibly empty) of field declarations, enclosed in parentheses. These field declarations are written in the normal way. As in a parameter list, no semicolon is written after the last declaration in the list. Somewhat confusingly the **case** does not have an associated **end**. Instead, given that the variant field always comes at the end of the record, the **end** of the record also serves to end the **case**. The fields that we have declared in the above **case** can be used exactly as if they had been declared

```
    hasnumber: Boolean;
    partnumber: integer;
    classcode: strength;
    partname: nameofpart;
```

The one proviso is that you must not, of course, try to refer to a field that is not there, such as the *partname* of a part for which *hasnumber* is *true*.

To avoid such catastrophes, you normally use an **if** or **case** statement to find out which variant is present. For example

```
var
    order: part;
begin
{   .
    .
    .
    . }
    if order.hasnumber then
        if order.classcode = delicate then
            writeln('Beware: it is delicate');
```

If you inadvertently write

```
if order.hasnumber then
    write(order.partname);
```

or even

```
write(order.partname);
```

on its own in a case where that field is non-existent, then the **Admirable Perkins** should catch you out, as the *partname* field would not be there. Here as always, or at least nearly always, Perkins' activities are a great help to us, because he prevents programs doing crazy things. (However you may well find that your compiler does not do the necessary checking, so the advantage is lost.)

Advantages of variants

The most obvious advantage of variant records is that they save storage. Two other aspects are just as important. There is the security, already mentioned, that prevents references to fields that do not exist. There is also the question of readability – once you get used to it: the record description gives a good deal of information about how the record is structured.

The restriction that the variant part of a record must come at the end is, in fact, no restriction. This is because variants can – naturally – be nested, so you can thus introduce several variants into a record, if you can stomach the idea.

An alternative form of variants

Finally, there is an alternative way of writing variants, which should act as a reward for Bill Mudd if he has managed to get this far. The alternative allows you to omit the discriminator field, with the result that the Admirable Perkins cannot keep tabs on what you are doing. It is called an 'undiscriminated union'. For example you could say that a field is either a real or an integer or a string of four characters, and Bill could set the field as, say, a character string, and then retrieve it as an integer, without Perkins being any the wiser. If you are used to programming in a so-called 'typeless' language such as BCPL (Richards & Whitby-Strevens, 1979), or even in assembly language, you might appreciate undiscriminated unions. You could define a record that consists of a single field that is the undiscriminated union of all data types that occupy a single word of your machine; this gives you the equivalent of a typeless variable. An array of these is like a machine store. The syntax is

```
type
{ Typical usage of a word on a 32-bit computer }
    fourcases = 1 .. 4
    word =
        record
            case fourcases of
                1: (
                    r: real
                    );
                2: (
                    i: integer
                    );
                3: (
                    str: packed array [1 .. 4] of char
                    );
                4: (
                    B: Boolean
                    );
        end;
    store = array [1 .. 1000] of word;
var
    w: word;
begin
    w.str := 'abcd';
    writeln('My compiler stores abcd as the integer', w.i);
```

Note that the discriminator after the **case** has no name, it is just a type.

Such facilities are useful for the dirty programming tricks that Bill likes to play, but, sad to say, most of us occasionally have to resort to dirty tricks to make our programs match real-world constraints, or interface with real-world devices.

The choice of the integers 1,2,3,4 in the above example is quite arbitrary, as we never actually set a discriminator. Given, however, that you have to enumerate the cases it is a natural sequence to use.

Name equivalence

Finally, it is worth repeating a specialized but important point made in the previous Chapter. Some compilers insist that, when you assign one variable to another, then if the two variables are declared separately, they must both have a data type with an identical *name*. It is not good enough declaring them both to be arrays of the same size or records with the same names of fields. (The only exception comes with simple types, where compatible types can be assigned to one another, e.g. a subrange of, say, integer can be assigned to an integer and vice-versa.) This strict rule is called *name equivalence*, and it applies both to explicit assignment and the implied assignment of an argument to a parameter. (See Welsh, Sneeringer & Hoare (1981) for a further discussion.) If you declare all your types in the **type** section of the program, thus giving them names, you will be safe. It is best to give names even to the data types of fields within records. Thus our *applicantb* is better than *applicanta*, because the latter has a name (*date*) for the data type of the field *birthdate*. As a result this field can safely be assigned to any other variable of type *date*.

CHAPTER 9

Input
and output

One of the greatest pleasures in life is conversation.

REV. SYDNEY SMITH

Modern education is often held to emphasize flamboyant and trendy subjects at the expense of basic skills. Pascal suffers in the same way. It is strong on data structures and the like but comparatively weak on the three R's: reading, riting, and rithmetic. Its rithmetic lacks an exponentiation operator, and, an omission felt by commercial programmers, decimal operations. Its reading and riting, i.e. its input and output, seem to be designed to help sell Bill's *BASIC from Pascal* book. It is not so much that Pascal's input/output is short on facilities; it is just that some fundamental things are difficult or impossible to do.

Categories of file

You have probably had the experience of trying to print a file and the printing coming out as gobbledegook. This may be because the file really contains gobbledegook, but often it is because the file is stored in an internal binary form that is not directly printable.

As you doubtless know, most computers store numbers in an internal binary encoding, which is different from the string of characters (digits, decimal points, etc.) we use to represent numbers. In fact the internal encoding of objects such as real numbers is a very elaborate one, and it takes a lot of computer time to convert, for example, between 2.397E–3 and the equivalent binary encoding.

Hence, to save conversion time, many computers have a facility for filing information in a binary form that is more or less a direct image of the encoding inside the computer store. These, then, are the files that print as gobbledegook.

Pascal offers both character and binary files. The former are the more common and are called *textfiles*.

In BASIC, when you refer to a file you use a channel number. If you omit this channel number the default input or output file is used. Thus you can use

PRINT X

to print on the default output file, or

PRINT #3: X

to print on the file corresponding to channel 3. An equivalent system applies for INPUT statements.

Pascal has a somewhat similar philosophy, except that the influence of Mr. 869704 is banished. Channel numbers are therefore replaced by identifiers, which are called *file variable*s, or, more simply, *files*. These identifiers are declared in the **var** section of the program in the normal way. They can, if desired, be local to a procedure, either as parameters or as local variables. The syntax for declaring file variables is illustrated by the following examples.

```
var
    ƒ1: file of char;
    ƒ2: file of integer;
    ƒ3: text;              { see below for explanation }
```

A file is a sequence of components that are all of the same data type. This data type is called the *component type*, and can be anything you like (even an array or record), though some Pascal implementations place restrictions on files of files.

A file declaration bears some similarity to an array declaration, and we shall pursue this similarity later. If, like *f*1 above, a file is of *char*, then the file is a textfile, i.e. the kind of file most familiar to us all. If the type associated with the file is anything other than *char* the file is a binary file. Because textfiles are the more frequent, Pascal has a built-in data type called *text*, which means **file of** *char*. Thus *f*3 above is, like *f*1, a textfile.

The names *input* and *output* are automatically assumed to be textfiles; they correspond to the default input and output files in much the same way as in BASIC, and nearly always correspond to your terminal. (The concept of 'file' is therefore generalized to include material typed at your terminal, as well as material in the computer's backing store. Good systems offer complete device-independence, as discussed in Chapter 3.)

The usage of file variables on input/output statements is also similar to the use of channel numbers in BASIC. A file variable can be written as an optional first argument to Pascal's *read* and *write* procedures. If the argument is omitted then *input* or *output* is assumed as appropriate. Thus the two statements

read(*x*, *y*);
read(*input*, *x*, *y*);

are equivalent, as are the two statements

write(*x*, *y* + 6, '*pig*');
write(*output*, *x*, *y* + 6, '*pig*');

Examples of the use of the file variables declared earlier are

read(*f*1, *x*, *y*);
read(*f*2, *x*, *y*); { *you can also read and write binary files* }
write(*f*3, *x*, *y*);

Data types on input/output

If a file is a textfile, then you can read from it items of input data that are of type *integer*, *real* or *char*. Items of numeric data in the textfile must be separated from one another by one or more spaces. (BASIC normally uses commas rather than spaces as separators.) Alternatively items of input data can be placed on separate lines. Obviously, each data item must be a constant of the appropriate type. If you supply the data 'xyz' when a real number is required you get an error. When a number is read, any leading spaces and/or 'newlines' are skipped over, the number is taken and the file is left positioned at the character beyond the number. When a *char* is read, a single character is taken – a space counts as a character just like anything else.

As an example of data formats, if the program contains the lines

var
    c: *char*;
    i: *integer*;
    r: *real*;

begin
    read(c, i, r);

then the corresponding input data can be

    x 23 9.7

or

    x
    23
    9.7

or

    x 23
    9.7

or, finally

    x23
    9.7

(This last example shows that no separator is needed between a character and a number.)

Note that the *read* statement automatically converts from external form (e.g. 9.7) to the internal binary form.

For output to a textfile, you can *write* the same types of item that you can *read*, i.e. *char*, *integer* or *real*. There are, in addition, two further data types you can write. Output of Booleans is Pascal's answer to the write-only store; you can write Booleans– they come out as *true* or *false* – but not read them. Likewise with strings, but you can fairly simply write a procedure to read a string character by character.

For files that are not textfiles, you can only read and write data items that are of the same data type as the component type of the file.

External file names

So far, so good; files in Pascal are much as you probably expected them to be.

The problems start when you wish to define the correspondence between the file names used in your program and the actual names of the files in your filing system. We shall call the latter *actual files* and the corresponding file variables within your program *external files* (as they refer to files that exist externally to the program). Most likely, actual files will be stored on a disc.

In BASIC the correspondence between actual files and external files (BASIC's channel numbers) is defined by a statement such as

    FILE #3: "SURVEYDATA"

In Pascal there is no equivalent to the FILE statement. Instead you must specify, on your program heading (i.e. the **program** construction at the very start), all the external files your program needs. This explains why for simple programs you write as your program heading

program *x*(*input, output*);

It means that the files *input* and *output* are to be known in the outside world. As we showed in Chapter 5, a program heading is somewhat analogous to a procedure heading. In the case of the program heading all the parameters are file names, and it is by this means that the program interacts with its outside environment.

Before explaining other external files, we shall make some points about the use of *input* and *output* on program headings. Some programs do not, in fact, have any input, and others do not take any input from the default *input* file. In these cases the parameter *input* can be omitted from the program heading. It is hard to imagine a program that does not use *output*. Even a program to copy one file to another, which would not use *output* for its normal output, might still need *output* for possible error messages. Some Pascal systems, in fact, insist that *output* is mentioned on the program heading.

External and actual correspondence

When your program uses external files other than *input* and *output* these too should appear on the program heading. For example

program *analyse*(*input, output, f*1);

For preferred rules concerning ordering of these external file names, see your local manual; in certain systems it would be most convenient to put *f*1 at the start of the list. Some Pascals allow you to write an asterisk after files that are only to be read; this protects against accidental writing. Given the above program heading, the name of the actual file corresponding to *f*1 is then defined by the command in your operating system which initiates a Pascal run. It might, for example, be

RUN *analyse*(,,SURVEYDATA)

or

RUN *analyse f*1 = SURVEYDATA

(Some systems use the more dramatic word 'EXECUTE' instead of 'RUN'.) Operating systems vary greatly, so you will need to consult your local manual. In most cases the default is that your terminal will be used for *input* and *output*, but you can override this if you wish. (In both our RUN examples, the files corresponding to *input* and *output* are not specified. This means that the defaults are to apply. If, instead, you want *input* and/or *output* to go elsewhere you can specify actual file names.)

In many operating systems the default rule for names other than *input* and *output* is that the actual name is the same as the name of the external file. In the above example the name *f*1 would, in the absence of an explicit specification, also serve as the actual name. Such systems are, however, by no means universal, and in general it should *not* be assumed that external file names correspond to actual ones (any more than the BASIC channel numbers do).

All external files, other than *input* and *output*, that you specify in the program heading should also be declared in the **var** section of the main program. Thus if the heading is

program *xxx(input, output, f*1, *f*2, *f*3);

then declarations of *f*1, *f*2 and *f*3, such as those given earlier in this Chapter, would be needed. The files *input* and *output*, however, must *not* be declared; they are already declared by default.

Inside your Pascal program you may create some temporary files which have no existence outside the program, or even, perhaps, outside a procedure to which the file is local. An example might arise in a sorting program, which creates an intermediate file containing a partial sort of its data. You do not need to worry about actual names for these temporary files.

The problem with Pascal's system for actual file names is that the number of actual files is fixed in advance by the number of external files on the program heading. Thus it is not possible to write, say, a merging program which merges an arbitrary number of files. (Nor is it possible to write a BASIC interpreter in Pascal, if your BASIC allows an arbitrary number of SAVEs and OLDs on different actual files.) Because this is such a severe restriction, some Pascal compilers have special extensions to get round the problem. Many extend the *reset* and *rewrite* statements, which we shall describe later.

Characteristics of files in Pascal

All files in Pascal are serial (sequential). There is no mechanism for random-access files (unless your compiler contains special extensions). This means that when you read a file you must start at the beginning and proceed component by component through the file. When you write a file you can only append to the end of the file – you cannot change anything already written, other than by starting from scratch and rewriting the whole file.

Associated with every file, therefore, is a point of scan, or, in Pascal terminology, a *window*, that is looking at a component of a file (or at the end of the file). You refer to the window of file *f* as *f*↑; its data type is the component type of the file, and it can be used like an ordinary variable. The value of *f*↑ is synonymous with the value of the current component.

The *get* and *put* procedures

If you want to perform input/output at a lower level of detail than with *read* and *write*, Pascal provides a number of built-in procedures which deal with the files at the window level. The most important procedures are *get*, which is used for input, and *put*, which is used for output.

The call

get(f);

advances the window of the file *f* to point at the next component.

The code

var
    tfile: **file of** *t*; { *where t is any type* }
    x: *t*; { *a variable of type t* }

```
begin
    x := tfile↑;
    get(tfile);
```

reads the value of the current component into *x*, and advances the window beyond the component. This is just what the *read* procedure does when called with *x* as argument. Hence the code above is the equivalent of

```
read(tfile, x);
```

Normally, you will perform all your input by using *read*, and not worry about *get*, but sometimes it is convenient to program at a lower level and actually use windows and *get*. Similar considerations apply to *write* and its corresponding low-level procedure *put*. (Some compilers follow the Pascal report in restricting *read* and *write* to textfiles, though the Pascal standard allows for binary files. If you have such a restricted compiler you will need to redo the banned *read*s and *write*s at the lower level – a slightly tiresome task, but not an onerous one. The task would need doing, for example, in the file-summing program shown later in this Chapter.)

Note that for textfiles, a *read* can do more than a *get*. If you read a real number, for instance, Pascal automatically *get*s all the characters that make up the number, and converts them to the internal binary form.

Corresponding to the input procedure *get* there is an output procedure *put*. The call

```
put(f);
```

adds the window *f*↑ to the end of the file *f*. You should assign something to the window before you do the *put*. The file *f* must be positioned at the end of the file at the time the *put* is performed. This is another way of saying that files must be written sequentially – you can only write by appending to the end.

The statement

```
write(tfile, x);
```

is equivalent to

```
tfile↑ := x;
put(tfile);
```

(Again, however, textfiles may be an exception. Writing, say, a real number to a textfile is more complicated than a single *put*, as it involves a conversion and the output of several characters.)

The following piece of program illustrates the use of *get* and *put*. It reads the *input* file until it finds the first occurrence of the character ':'; all the text passed over is copied to the *output* file.

```
while input↑ < > ':' do
begin
    output↑ := input↑;
    put(output);
    get(input);
end;
```

As it stands, the above program contains two defects, which we shall explain later. We shall refer back, therefore, to this colon-searching program.

If you wish to do something 'questionable' like reading a file using *get* and then writing at the end of the same file using *put*, consult your local Pascal manual. What you can and cannot do is more often dictated by the local operating system than by Pascal's own rules.

Initializing files

Pascal provides a built-in procedure

rewrite(f);

which prepares a file for writing; this is done by destroying the previous contents of the file (if any), and positioning the window at the start of the file. In this case the start of the file is also the end, because the file is null.

There is a similar procedure

reset(f);

which prepares a file for reading. This positions the window at the start of the file, ready for reading. In this case the start of the file is not normally the end, or there would be nothing to read.

Before using any file that you have declared you should *reset* it or *rewrite* it as appropriate. The built-in files *input* and *output* are, however, automatically prepared for reading and writing (respectively), and you should never *reset* or *rewrite* these.

"All very logical," said Bill, with what appeared to be a touch of sarcasm in his voice. "I don't understand why you do a *rewrite* to prepare for a write, but not a *reread* to prepare for a read. The very name 'rewrite' also seems a tiny bit strange: you *rewrite* before you *write*. Doubtless if I was as clever as Professor Primple I would understand these things."

The *eof* function

You often want to read input data until it runs out, i.e. until you reach the end of the input file. In BASIC the end of a file may be detected by a statement such as IF END. Pascal provides a built-in Boolean function

eof(f)

which is *true* only if the file *f* is positioned at the end of a file. Hence you can only *put* or *write* to a file if *eof* is *true*, and you can only *get* or *read* if *eof* is *false*.

One defect of our colon-searching program is that it would read past the end of the file if no colon was found. It would be better to use the *eof* function to test for this error condition and, if it arose, give a decent error message.

The following complete program illustrates the use of files and *eof*. The program adds together a sequence of real numbers in the input file; when the end of the file is reached, the program prints the total sum and stops.

```
program sumfile(datafile, output);
{ Program to sum all the components of a file }
var
    datafile: file of real;
    sum: real;
    x: real;
begin
    reset(datafile);
    sum := 0;
    while not eof(datafile) do
    begin
        read(datafile, x);
        sum := sum + x;
    end;
    writeln('Sum =', sum);
end.
```

This example illustrates several points made earlier. It shows how an external file, such as *datafile*, appearing in the program heading, needs to be declared among all the other variables at the start of the program. The file *output*, on the other hand, is not declared.

This program does not use the file *input*, which has therefore been omitted from the program heading. It would not have mattered, however, if *input* had been redundantly included in the program heading. Many people make

```
program xxx(input, output);
```

the first line of all their programs (provided they do not use external files) irrespective of whether *input* is actually used.

The file *datafile* is declared as a file of *real*. The program could be adjusted to work on a textfile rather than a binary file by declaring datafile as

```
datafile: text;
```

There are, however, problems with the use of *eof* on textfiles. Later in this Chapter we shall define a function *texteof*, which should be used in place of *eof* in the above program if input is from a textfile.

As regards the way the program works, this should be easy to follow. It simply reads data, accumulating the sum, until the end of the file is reached. Note that the program works even if *datafile* is null.

Files as parameters

It is instructive to rewrite the above program as a procedure, which takes a file as a parameter and prints the sum of the components of that file.

We shall assume that we want to sum three separate files, so that it becomes natural to use a procedure. The program to accomplish this is as follows

```
program sum3files(file1, file2, file3, output);
{ Sums the components of each of three files }
type
    realfile = file of real;
var
    file1, file2, file3: realfile;

procedure sumfile(var datafile: realfile);
{ Prints the sum of all the components of datafile }
var
    sum: real;
    x: real;
begin
    reset(datafile);
    sum : = 0;
    while not eof(datafile) do
    begin
        read(datafile, x);
        sum : = sum + x;
    end;
    writeln('Sum=', sum);
end; { sumfile }

begin { main program }
    sumfile(file1);
    sumfile(file2);
    sumfile(file3);
end.
```

Notice how the parameter to *sumfile* has been declared as a **var** parameter. If this were omitted, then the first action on

sumfile(file1);

would be to copy the argument to the parameter. This would require the copying of the whole of *file1*. This is such an outrageous thing to do that Pascal forbids it altogether. File parameters must always be **var** parameters.

The program also serves to illustrate a problem raised earlier. This is that all external files must be declared in the program heading, and thus there is no way in Pascal to create a file name dynamically. This means that there is no equivalent of BASIC's

```
PRINT "TYPE THE NAME OF THE FILE TO BE USED:";
INPUT S$
FILE #3: S$
```

(though, as we have said, your local Pascal may have an extension – perhaps an extra parameter to *reset* and *rewrite* – to help achieve the same effect). Hence, if we wished to sum four files rather than three, we would have to change the above program in three ways

- to add *file*4 to the program heading
- to declare *file*4
- to apply *sumfile* to *file*4

Operations on files

"What if I wanted to apply *sumfile* to *input*?" said Bill, the gleam in his eyes belying the apparent innocence of the question.

Unfortunately the answer is that the program would fail, because *sumfile* *reset*s its parameter and you cannot *reset input*. Nor can you include a test within the procedure such as

if *datafile* < > *input* **then** *reset(datafile)*;

You cannot compare file names.

This is somewhat reminiscent of records. You cannot do anything to records except assign them. Files are, however, a shade worse. You cannot even assign one file to another. All you can do is pass them as **var** parameters, use them as arguments to built-in procedures such as *get*, and reference the current window.

Cockneys, who pronounce 'fail' as 'file', are perhaps thinking of Pascal.

Files and arrays

We have already observed that a file declaration has some similarity to an array declaration, as the declarations

a: **array** [1 . . 100] **of** *real*;
f: **file of** *real*;

show.

If we mention the differences between the two concepts, this will reinforce some of the properties of Pascal's files.

Firstly it can be seen that a file, unlike an array, can be of unlimited size, subject, of course, to the size of your machine and its backing store. This does not mean, however, that if you redeclare all your arrays to be files then all your problems will go away. Problems arise because you can only read files sequentially, and, worse still, only write them sequentially. This means that even if you only change a single element you must rewrite the whole file.

Secondly, if you intersperse reading and writing you must continually *reset* and *rewrite* the file.

Thus in only a few programs can you conveniently use files to store big arrays. However if your local Pascal offers random-access files, and you do not care about portability, the opportunities are much greater.

Special properties of textfiles

So far most of what we have said applies equally to textfiles and binary files. The only extra facility we noted for textfiles was the ability to read and write various different data types and convert them to internal form.

Textfiles possess a further important property: they are divided into lines. These lines are separated by 'newline' characters. In some languages such newlines are real characters that you can manipulate like any others. In other languages, like BASIC, the newline is a hypothetical character. Pascal takes an intermediate view: the newline counts as a character, but when you read it you get a space. Thus if the input data on the textfile *input* consists of the lines

```
23
4
x ...
```

and you execute the program

```
for k := 1 to 5 do
begin
    write(input↑);
    get(input);
end;
```

With the window initially positioned at the character '2', your output consists of the five characters '2', '3', space, '4', space. The window finishes pointing at the 'x' character.

This reveals the second defect of our colon-searching program: as it copies the input to the output, all the newlines are turned to spaces.

Although the newline appears to you as a space, there is a means of detecting its presence. This is done by the built-in function *eoln*, which is similar to the *eof* function. The *eoln* function returns the value *true* only if the window is positioned at the end of a line.

The *eoln* function can be used to get around one of Pascal's limitations. The program fragment shown below reads a line of characters and assembles them into a string. If thus achieves the effect of reading a string. The code, which both inputs a string and prints it out, is as follows

```
const
    linemaxlength = 80;
var
    inputline: packed array [1 .. linemaxlength] of char;
    k: integer;
    linelength: 0 .. linemaxlength;
begin
    for k := 1 to linemaxlength do { blank out the line }
        inputline[k] := ' ';
    linelength := 0;
    while not eoln(input) do
    begin
        if linelength < linemaxlength then
            linelength := linelength + 1
        else
            { ... give an error ... };
        read(inputline[linelength]);
    end;
```

{ *Now pass over the newline character, so that the next input comes on a fresh*
   line }
    get(input); { *alternatively (see later): readln;* }

{ *Now write the line just read* }
    writeln(inputline);

{ *The above writes all the spaces at the end of inputline.*
  The statements below are an improvement, avoiding these spaces
    for *k* := 1 **to** *linelength* **do**
      write(inputline[k]);
    writeln;
}

The *writeln* and *readln* procedures

In BASIC there is a big difference between

    PRINT X;
and PRINT X

As you know, the latter terminates the current line – it outputs a newline, if you like – whereas the former allows further output on the same line.

In Pascal, as we have already indicated in Chapter 6, the equivalents to the above BASIC statements are

    write(x);
and *writeln(x);*

Thus the procedure *writeln* terminates a line whereas *write* does not. Just as you can use

    PRINT

as a statement on its own in BASIC, you can use

    writeln;

on its own in Pascal. A sequence of statements such as

    writeln; writeln; writeln;

is useful for writing a series of blank lines. Like *write*, *writeln* has an optional file name as its first argument. Assuming *f* is a file name, the following are examples

    writeln(f, x);
    writeln(f); writeln(f); { *two blank lines on file f* }

Pascal also supports a built-in procedure *readln*, which has no direct equivalent in BASIC. Just as *writeln* adds a newline after the last of its arguments has been output, thus causing further output to appear on a fresh line, *readln*, after the data for its last argument has been read, skips over the rest of the current line, so that further data is taken from the next line. Thus if *k* is an integer variable, and the statement

readln(k);

is executed with the input data

23 24 *is lost*
x . . .

then *k* will be set to 23, the data ' 24 is lost' is skipped over, and the window is left pointing at the character *x* at the start of the next line.

Note that in a statement such as

readln(a, b, c);

it is quite legal for the data for *a*, *b* and *c* to be on a single line or on three separate lines, as is normal for a *read*. The only difference about *readln* is that it skips to beyond the next newline after the value supplied for *c*.

Like *writeln*, *readln* can be used on its own, without an argument list, to skip to the beginning of the next line.

As an adjunct to *writeln*, Pascal provides a built-in procedure

page(f)

which starts a new page on the file *f*.

The procedures *readln*, *writeln* and *page* can only be used on textfiles.

End-of-file on textfiles

In many operating systems, the end of a textfile can only come after a complete line. You can think of end-of-file as an imaginary character that comes at the start of a line.

This has a bearing on the use of the *eof* function on textfiles. When you test for *eof* you should have the window positioned at the potential start of a line. The following lines of program will therefore not work.

read(x);
if *eof(input)* **then** { . . . } ;

This is because *read* will leave the window at the character beyond the number just read. Assuming the user supplied the line

23

the window would be pointing at the newline character beyond the '3'. (Remember that if you actually look at this character it turns into a space.) Therefore *eof* will always be false.

To remedy this you should read the newline character, so that the window gets positioned at the start of the next line. This can be done by *read(x, nextchar)*;

where *nextchar* is declared as a *char* variable, or, better, by

readln(x);

The latter is an improvement because it absorbs any spaces, or indeed any other characters, that follow the value of *x*, but it is only applicable if the item of data supplied for *x* is known to be at the end of a line. (Otherwise the 'other characters' skipped over might be vital data.)

There is, however, a solution that is neater and more reliable than either of these two alternatives. This is to write a function *texteof*, which is equivalent to 'skip over spaces (if any) until a non-space character or the end of a line is reached, and then perform *eof*'. Once this function has been defined you can use it freely in place of *eof* whenever you are scanning a textfile in contexts where spaces are not significant. It is a good example of creating a tool to perform what is otherwise a difficult task.

The function *texteof* is defined as follows

```
function texteof(var f: text): Boolean;
{ Scans along file f until a non-space or the end of a line is reached;
  returns the value true if f is then at eof }
var
    stopscan: Boolean; { false if we wish to scan ahead for spaces }
begin
    repeat { loop to scan over any spaces }
        stopscan := true; { the default }
        if not eof(f) then
            if f↑ = ' ' then
            begin
                stopscan := eoln(f); { do not scan beyond end of line }
                get(f);
            end;
    until stopscan;
    texteof := eof(f);
end; { texteof }
```

Interactive input/output

The early implementors of Pascal visualized input/output devices as card-readers, line printers, and the like. Any attempt to interact using a terminal met with disaster. Even an attempt to prepare a Pascal program on any medium other than cards was fraught with dangers, such as having everything beyond column 72 taken as a sequence number. Some of these compilers are still around, driving their users to drink or BASIC.

We shall mention a few of the problems, so you can laugh now before the tears come later.

One problem is that some Pascal compilers keep output in largish 'buffers' of, say, 1024 characters. Output comes out only when the corresponding output buffer is full, or the program has finished execution. Conversations with Pascal programs then take on a curious air. You hammer away at your input, and the computer remains silent. Then suddenly it springs into life, spouting 1024 characters at you, and answering questions you typed in long previously. (These buffers cause problems when programs fail due to errors; you often lose the last incomplete buffer, with the result that debugging becomes a fine guessing game.) The buffers are, of course, designed to make transfers to and from magnetic tape or disc more efficient, and the interactive fiasco is an unfortunate side effect.

Buffers apply to input as well as output. Many Pascal systems actually process interactive input in terms of lines, with the result that input is not examined until the RETURN key is pressed. Other Pascal systems – mainly on micros – offer so-called *raw mode* input, whereby each character typed by an interactive user is processed immediately. Consult your local manual for details; you may well find, in any case, that interactive input is treated in a non-standard way.

Another problem arises with the definition of *read*. Pascal advances the window to the character beyond the one last read. If this last character is at the end of a line – or if you have used *readln* rather than *read* – then Pascal advances the window to the start of the next line. Many Pascal compilers ask you at this point to input the next line. This is done before the line you previously typed has been processed. The result, in a steady state, is that you are always typing one line ahead of the one that has just been processed. In consequence, if your program produces prompts, these will apply to the line you had previously typed. Thus a conversation might run as follows (where what the machine types is in lower case)

> ... JOHN
> *what is your name?* 26
> *how old are you?* NOT PASCAL
> *what is the best programming language for i/o?*

Things get worse still if your psychic powers fail, and you get a reply wrong. All in all, one of the greatest pleasures in life is somewhat diluted.

Similar problems arise if your program prints a reply to each line of input, e.g.

> .
> .
> .
> 64
> *is not a power of two*
> 23
> *is a power of two*
> 32
> *is not a power of two*

(Each answer relates to the previous input but one.)

We shall call this the *out-of-phase* problem. If your Pascal compiler presents such problems you may be able to write somewhat tricky procedures that will surmount the difficulties. See Kaye (1980) for a good discussion of the mechanisms involved. Alternatively switch to a compiler that has paid some thought to the interactive user.

A last problem with interactive input is that Pascal assumes that the person at the terminal is perfect, and makes no mistakes. If data is of the wrong format – for example a letter where a number is expected – Pascal gives an error message and terminates the run altogether.

A conversation on a computer-aided learning program might run as follows. (We assume that the out-of-phase problem has been solved.)

> *What is two plus two?*
> 5
> *Sorry, Jimmy, this is not quite right, try again.*
> *What is two plus two?*
> $ (Jimmy forgets to press the shift key for '4')
> *Error in input data*
> *Halted in procedure readreply*
> *End of run.*

The keys of the terminal are then moistened with Jimmy's tears.

There is no way round this problem (unless your Pascal has a special non-standard extension) other than writing your own procedures to take input one character at a time, and convert it to numeric form where necessary. If there are any errors, you can then give a friendly message and ask the user to try again.

Interactive testing for end-of-file

Even if you have a good interactive compiler, you still need to exercise care if you want to conquer completely the out-of-phase problem. The following code shows the problem

```
sum : = 0;
while not eof(input) do
begin
    write('Sum so far =', sum, '; type the next number:');
    readln(x);
    sum : = sum + x;
end;
writeln('Total sum = ', sum);
```

This program uses *readln*, as we recommended earlier, because *eof* then works properly. (Use of the *texteof* function might have been better, but it would make this discussion more complicated.)

Even if your interactive compiler is clever enough not to get out-of-phase because of *readln* itself, it still gets out-of-phase because of a logical problem associated with the *eof* function. The only way Pascal can tell if there is an end-of-file is to ask you for another line of input and see if there is one. (We assume an end-of-file at a terminal is indicated by typing some special character at the start of the line.) Thus the user is asked to type a line every time **while not** *eof(input)* is executed. This line is then used by the *readln* statement that comes three lines below. The effect is that the user is asked to supply his input line at a slightly earlier stage than a casual glance at the program would indicate. The problem is that there is a *write* that comes after the *eof*, but before the *readln*. This *write* is executed, therefore, after a line has been input, but before that line has been processed. The familiar result is that input gets out of phase, e.g.

> 23
> *Sum so far =   0; type the next number:* 46
> *Sum so far = 23; type the next number: (END-OF-FILE)*
> *Total sum = 69*

This is a logical problem, not a problem of your Pascal compiler, and the only way round it is to rewrite your program so that the *write* comes before the *eof*. In the above case the somewhat messy result is

> *sum* : = 0;
> *write('Sum so far = 0; type the next number:');*
> **while not** *eof(input)* **do**
> **begin**
>   *readln(x);*
>   *sum* : = *sum* + *x;*
>   *write('Sum so far =', sum, '; type the next number:');*
> **end;**
> *writeln('Total sum =', sum);*

Given that interactive testing for *eof* will cause you problems, the best advice is to think very carefully before using it. Would it be better to reformulate your program so that *eof* is avoided? One alternative is to keep asking the interactive user whether he has any more data, and to stop when he says no. Another is to use some special value to act as a terminator for a particular set of data – the value zero is often suitable.

The same extreme wariness should be applied to interactive use of *eoln*.

Output formats

As the final major topic in this Chapter, we shall consider *output formats*. We should confess at this point that the *write*s in all the previous examples in this book have used very crude output formats, and the results in many cases would be unpleasant to look at; Pascal provides a means to do better.

Similar, but rather more powerful, facilities are present in those BASICs that allow a USING clause on a PRINT. The USING clause applies to an entire PRINT statement, but Pascal's format control facilities are applied to individual arguments to *write* or *writeln*. The most useful Pascal facility is the ability to append, to an item to be printed, an integer representing a *minimum field width*. The following example illustrates the syntax

> *writeln('Totals for case ', caseno: 2, ' are ', suma: 10, sumb);*

As can be seen, a colon is written after each item that is to have a minimum field width. In this example, *caseno* (which we assume to be an integer) has a minimum field width of two; this means it would normally be printed as two characters. The rule is quite straightforward if *caseno* is between 10 and 99. If *caseno* consists of a single digit, the rule is that it is right-aligned, i.e. a space is put on the front. If *caseno* is greater than 99, then it obviously will not fit into two characters. This is, however, not normally an error in Pascal; instead the value is printed using as few characters as possible. Remember that the integer 2 represents the *minimum* field width, not necessarily the one actually used. Thus if you want an item always to be printed in the fewest possible number of characters you can give it a minimum field width of 1.

Minimum field widths can be applied to items of any data type, though they are most often applied to integers and reals. If you omit the minimum field width – as we have done on all our examples until we reached this Section – you get an implementation-defined default width for the data type. See your local Pascal manual for details. In our above example, *suma* is printed with a width of 10, but *sumb* is printed with the default width associated with its data type.

In practice these default widths often turn out to be large, with the result that, if we had omitted the ':2' after *caseno*, an output line might appear as

Totals for case   4 are ...

It looks as if Mr. 869704 has persuaded compiler writers that output usually consists of widely separated columns of figures rather than a readable combination of text and numbers.

Fraction length

If a minimum field width is present this may be followed by a further colon and another integer, which is called the *fraction length*, e.g.

writeln('Sum=', suma: 8: 3, ' *units.');*

If a fraction length is present, the value to be printed must be a real number. In the above example the variable *suma* is printed with a minimum field width of 8 and a fraction length of 3. The latter means that three digits are to follow the decimal point. Thus, if *suma* has the value 12.34567, then the output would be

Sum=   12.346 units.

Notice that two spaces are printed on the front of the value of *suma*, thus ensuring the field width reaches the minimum of 8.

In fact the presence of the fraction length changes the way real numbers are printed. If there is no fraction length the value comes out in 'floating-point' notation, e.g.

$1.2345670000E+01$

Thus the fraction length is certainly a good guy, because he makes numbers come out in what is, to most of us, a much more readable form.

To summarize, the defaults that you get if you omit the minimum field width or the fraction length are usually the last thing that you would really want.

Further points

Obviously the format control facilities are only applicable if output is going to a textfile rather than a binary file.

The Pascal format control facilities actually have one advantage over the USING clause in BASIC. This is that the minimum field width and fraction length can be expressions whose values may change during a run. As a somewhat absurd example, the statement

> **for** $k := 1$ **to** 5 **do**
>   *writeln(k: k);*

would produce the output

```
1
 2
  3
   4
    5
```

More practically, these format controls can be defined using named constants, thus making changes easier, e.g.

> **const**
>   *casewidth* = 2;
> **var**
>   *caseno: integer;*
> **begin**
> {   .
>   .
>   . }
>   *writeln('Totals for case ', caseno: casewidth, ' are ... ');*

As a final point concerning formats, note that the Pascal statement

> *write(a, b, c);*

is akin to

> PRINT A; B; C;

in BASIC, rather than to

> PRINT A, B, C,

In other words Pascal does not insert extra spaces between items to be printed. This means that you usually have to put spaces on the beginning and/or end of strings that are interspersed with numbers. For example *writeln('Case'*, *caseno*: 2, *'result'*);

would, if *caseno* had the value of 18, produce the line

*Case*18*result*

Hence the above statement would be better specified as

writeln('Case ', *caseno*: 2, *' result'*);

If positive numbers are printed without format control, a space is printed for the sign (whereas a minus is printed on the front of negative numbers); thus there is no necessity for an extra space at the end of a preceding string.

Imprisoned data types

We outlined earlier the data types that could be input and output on textfiles. In this last Section we shall say more about the unhappy data types that are imprisoned inside Pascal, and cannot be input and output.

Prominent among the prisoners are the user-defined types. If you go back to the *slimmer* program of Chapter 7, you may remember that it had a type *day* that represented the days of the week. It also contained a variable *today* of type *day*. The program could be improved by outputting the value of *today* in the table of results. However the statement

write(today);

would not print the value of *today*, which might, say, be *tuesday*; instead the compiler would give an error message. If you really want to output the value of an object of type *day*, the best way to do it is to write a procedure. This might take the form

```
procedure writeday(d: day);
{ Writes the day of the week represented by d }
begin
   case d of
      monday:
         write('Monday');
      tuesday:
         write('Tuesday');
      wednesday:
         write('Wednesday');
      thursday:
         write('Thursday');
      friday:
         write('Friday');
      saturday:
         write('Saturday');
      sunday:
         write('Sunday');
   end;
end; { writeday }
```

These procedures are highly tedious to write. Their only merit is that if you have a friend or relation who is frightfully eager to help, but not much good at programming, then these procedures are ideal fodder and might result in your getting a bit of peace.

A corresponding input procedure would be worse still, as the names of the days have to be read and assembled character by character. It is unlikely that Aunty Amy or little Willy would manage to get the procedure right.

It is, indeed, a great shame that user-defined types are prisoners, as they would be even more useful otherwise.

Also among the prisoners are records, though these can squeeze in or out if treated one field at a time. This maltreatment of records would come as a big surprise to readers familiar with such languages as COBOL, where a central purpose of records is to define input/output formats.

You can, of course, input or output any data type if you use a binary file of that type, but such files are not readable by mortals, just by computer programs.

Graphics

For many people, computing without the use of graphics is like summer without cricket. Yet, as we have said already, Pascal has no graphics facilities, nor even elementary facilities for moving a cursor. Because this is such a shattering omission, many compilers have added their own non-standard graphics facilities. All we can do here is to refer you to your local Pascal manual.

Summary

You have probably got the impression, after reading this Chapter, that getting anything in or out of your Pascal program is like going round the Royal Saint George's golf course equipped only with a putter. Do not be too despondent. You can usually complete your task in the end, particularly if your Pascal contains reasonable extensions, and particularly if you build your own tools to help get over Pascal's bunkers.

There remains, nevertheless, a feeling that your task is a lot harder than it need be.

CHAPTER 10

Sets

All you think about is sets.

CONDEMNATION OF ADOLESCENT PASCAL PROGRAMMER

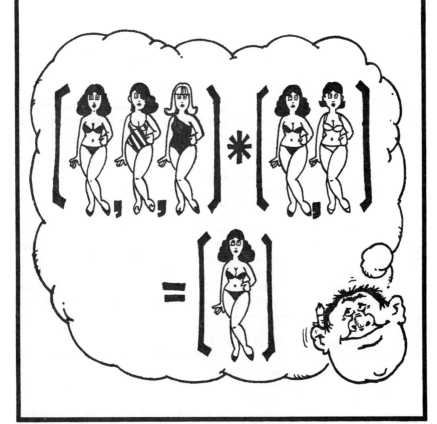

Having waded in the murky waters of input/output, we shall now return to a bright, clear pool. Instead of a long complicated Chapter, we now have a short and, it is hoped, simple one.

We are returning again to the topic of data types, and shall describe a new one which should change the way you think about some of your programs.

Introduction to sets

You can, in Pascal, define a data type that is a set of objects of some other data type. The latter is called the *base type* of the set. The base type of a set can be any simple type except real. It is usually a user-defined type, a subrange type, or *char*.

Few well-known programming languages other than Pascal support sets, and even with Pascal some early compilers placed onerous restrictions on the size of sets. The result is that sets are ignored by some Pascal programmers. This is a pity as sets can be incredibly useful, and can achieve a great deal towards making your program a closer description of the problem being solved.

An example of a set

Our first example of a set has a user-defined type as the base type. This user-defined type is a sequence of names of programming languages. The set is therefore a set of programming languages. It is defined thus

```
type
    languages = (Pascal, BASIC, BCPL, Simula, Algol60, Algol68,
                COBOL);
    knownlanguages = set of languages;
```

From the above you can see that to define a set you write **set of** followed by the base type. Given this declaration you can then use the data type in the normal way and, in particular, can declare variables to be of that data type, for example

```
var
    Primplelanguages: knownlanguages;
    Muddlanguages: knownlanguages;
    knowall, hopelesskins: knownlanguages;
```

Variables of the data type *knownlanguages* can take as their value any subset of the full set. At one extreme this subset can be null (the *empty set*), or, at the other extreme, it can be the complete set. Thus our set can be used to represent the set of programming languages known by a given person.

When you want to assign a value to a *knownlanguages* variable, you can use a *set constructor*. A set constructor is written by listing the desired set elements and enclosing the list in square brackets, e.g.

```
Primplelanguages := [Pascal, BCPL];
{ As set members can be written in any order, the above can also be written:
    Primplelanguages := [BCPL, Pascal]; }
Muddlanguages := [BASIC];
hopelesskins := []; { a null set }
knowall := [Pascal, BASIC, BCPL, Simula, Algol60, Algol68, COBOL];
```

There are, in fact, thousands of programming languages in existence, though only a dozen or so are well known. If we extended our data type *languages* to consist of, say, 100 languages it would become very tedious to write the set constructor to assign to *knowall*. To alleviate this, Pascal allows elements making up a set constructor to be specified by subranges of the base type. Thus we could write

knowall: = [*Pascal . . COBOL*];

As *Pascal* is the first value in the base type and *COBOL* is the last, this is equivalent to specifying all the values in the base type.

The following are two further examples

knowsmost: = [*Pascal . . BCPL, Algol60 . . COBOL*]; { *all except Simula* }
knowssome: = [*Pascal . . BCPL, Algol60, COBOL*];

A set is somewhat akin to a Boolean array in that each possible set member may be present or not; in other words its presence may be *true* or *false*. Carrying this idea further, a set is equivalent to the 'bit-string' found in assembly languages and some high-level languages, i.e. a sequence of values 1 (or *true*) and 0 (or *false*). Pascal sets are, however, much better than bit-strings because they make the program easier to read by banishing the influence of Mr. 869704 or, in this case, Mr. 11010100010101001000.

Operations on sets

Sets are not quite the second class citizens that some other Pascal data types are. Granted you cannot input them or output them, but at least there are some operators you can apply to sets. In particular, you can apply the operators ' + ', ' − ' and ' * '. You can probably guess the meanings of these operators when applied to sets from their meanings in arithmetic. Thus the set

$x + y$

consists of the set whose elements are either elements of x or elements of y or elements of both. The technical term for this is the *set union*. Alternatively, if you persist in thinking of sets as bit-strings a ' + ' is a logical 'or' ('*' will turn out to be the logical 'and'). In our example, the union

Primplelanguages + Muddlanguages

is the set

[*Pascal, BCPL, BASIC*]

and the union of any of our variables with *knowall* remains as the set of all our languages.

The minus operator means the *set difference*. Thus

$x - y$

consists of the set whose elements belong to x but not to y. In our example

knowall − Primplelanguages

is the set

[*BASIC, Simula, Algol*60, *Algol*68, *COBOL*]

Finally the operator ' * ' means the *set intersection*. This is such that

$x * y$

is the set whose elements belong to both x and y. In our example

*Primplelanguages * Muddlanguages*

is the empty set. On the other hand the intersection of *knowall* with any set z is identical to the value of the set z.

You should be able to think of examples where these operators on sets are useful. In our particular case, the union and intersection of *knownlanguage*s would be useful in a program to assign programming teams to given programming tasks which require a knowledge of certain languages.

Relational operations on sets

As well as ' + ', ' − ' and ' * ', you can apply relational operators to sets. The operators work as follows

- $x = y$ is *true* when x and y are identical sets
- $x <> y$ is *true* when x and y are not identical sets
- $x <= y$ is *true* if all elements of x are also elements of y
- $x >= y$ is *true* if all elements of y are also elements of x
- the operators ' > ' and ' < ' cannot be applied to sets

Given these rules, the relation

*Primplelanguages * Muddlanguages = hopelesskins*

is *true*, because both sides of the equals sign are empty sets. Moreover

[*BASIC, Simula*] = [*Simula, BASIC*]

is true, because the ordering of set elements is immaterial. As a third example

knowall >= *x*

is *true* for any set of *languages* x.

A further example, whose initial impact is surprising, is that

> *Muddlanguages* > = *Primplelanguages*
> and *Primplelanguages* > = *Muddlanguages*

are both *false*. Thus beware of carrying your thinking about relations between numbers directly over to relations between sets.

Finally, not only can you use four of the existing relational operators on sets, but you also have a new operator: **in**. This is such that

> *e* **in** *x*

is *true* if *e* is an element of the set *x*. The data type of *e* must be the same as the base type of the set *x*. In our example

> *BASIC* **in** *Primplelanguages*

is *false*, because Primple certainly does not admit to knowing **BASIC**.

Expressions within set constructors

In our examples so far, the elements within set constructors have been constants. They can actually be any expressions, as illustrated by

```
var
    x: set of 1 .. 31;
    p, q: integer;
begin
{   ·
    ·
    · }
    x := [p, q − 1 .. q + 3,  19,  20];
{   ·
    ·
    · }
    x := x + [p .. q];
{   ·
    ·
    · }
```

If *q* is less than *p* then [*p* .. *q*] is, of course, the empty set.

A complete example with characters

Sets are also useful for simplifying Boolean expressions that involve lots of **or** operations. We shall show an example of this using a set with *char* as base type. This is, in fact, one of the most popular base types and our example perhaps shows why.

```
program countchars(input, output);
{ Counts, within the input text:
    1. the number of letters or digits
    2. the number of punctuation characters ('.' or ',' or ';' or ':') }

var
    letterdigitcount: 0 .. maxint;
    punctuationcount: 0 .. maxint;
    currentchar: char;

begin
    letterdigitcount := 0;
    punctuationcount := 0;
    while not eof(input) do
    begin
        read(currentchar);
{ The statement below assumes the character set is such that all the letters
    have adjacent codes -- and similarly for the digits }
        if currentchar in ['a' .. 'z', 'A' .. 'Z', '0' .. '9'] then
            letterdigitcount := letterdigitcount + 1;
        if currentchar in ['.', ',', ';', ':'] then
            punctuationcount := punctuationcount + 1;
    end;
    writeln('Number of letters or digits is', letterdigitcount);
    writeln('Number of punctuation characters is', punctuationcount);
end.
```

This program does not use variables of set data type. All it uses are set constructors and the **in** facility; these two, however, certainly pull their weight in making the program easier to write and understand.

A second complete example

Our second complete example shows a program that relates to a dartboard. A game that an extreme amateur or an extreme drunkard can complete in a reasonable amount of time is as follows: hit, in any order, all the numbers from 1 to 20.

The following program inputs scores and prints a message when all the numbers have been hit.

```
program dartcover(input, output);
{ Keeps reading numbers until each of the numbers 1 to 20 has occurred at least
    once }
var
    hitnumbers: set of 1 .. 20;
    score: 1 .. 50; { a dartboard also contains 25 and 50 }
```

```
begin
    hitnumbers := []; { initially the empty set }
    repeat
        read(score);
        if  score < = 20  then
            hitnumbers := hitnumbers + [score];
    until  hitnumbers = [1 . . 20];
    writeln('*** SUCCESS: you have covered all the numbers');
end.
```

The interesting line is the one that resets *hitnumbers*. Notice that the ' + ' operator, when applied to sets, must have sets as both its operands. Thus the second operand must be [*score*], which is a set containing one element, the value of *score*. The statement

hitnumbers : = *hitnumbers* + *score*;

would be *wrong*, because *score* is not a set. Doubtless you will, like most of us, keep forgetting this rule when you come to write a program. However, perhaps the above example will jog your memory when you puzzle over the syntax error you get.

Disparate sets

Just as, within one program, you can employ any number of arrays of different shapes and types, you can also employ any number of sets of different base types. Thus our variable *Primplelanguages* could appear in the same program as *hitnumbers*. What you cannot do, however, is to apply set operations to disparate types, e.g.

Primplelanguages + *hitnumbers*

or

Primplelanguages = *hitnumbers*

Such operations are meaningless and will rightly be stamped upon by Perkins.

Restrictions on sets

Some early Pascal compilers, as we have mentioned, had severe restrictions on the size of sets. Typically a set was restricted to a small number of elements, 60 say. As almost every character set has more than 60 characters, this made **set of** *char* impossible. Often the restriction was still more crushing. Types such as

x = **set of** 58 . . 62; { *upper limit* > 60 }
y = **set of** '*a*' . . '*z*';

were not allowed. The reason was that the bounds of subranges must be between 0 and 59, or, in the case of *char*, the internal codes must be in this range. Most character sets do not satisfy this restriction on *char*. If the restriction applies, our example of testing for letters or digits might not work, because the character being tested and/or the elements of the set constructor might be out of range.

Hopefully, happier days are now with us, and the older compilers are being replaced by ones whose writers appreciate the true value of sets. Nevertheless there is still likely to be some restriction on the size of sets, for good implementation reasons. It is unlikely that you will be allowed to say

bigset = **set of** *integer*;

because the number of possible integers is very large indeed. In fact any base type involving negative or large positive integers is likely to be banned.

Perhaps the most important boundary on the size of sets is whether they can encompass the character set, normally 128 or 256 characters. If your compiler writers have made the effort to achieve this, make sure you cash in on their labours by exploiting sets to their full potential.

Other operations on sets

"I notice there are no built-in functions that work on sets," said Bill. "Nothing to count the number of elements, for example. I can see that sets are like most other things in Pascal: beautiful objects that are absolutely ideal provided you don't want to use them in real programs."

There are, indeed, no built-in functions on sets, but this is actually a *good* feature of Pascal. As we have said, leviathan languages are not what the user needs.

With operations on sets, Pascal is successfully lean and supple. Bill's problem of counting the elements of a set, for example, can be achieved as follows – we assume the set to be counted is *Muddlanguages*.

count := 0;
for *k* := *Pascal* **to** *COBOL* **do**
    if *k* **in** *Muddlanguages* **then**
        count := *count* + 1;

CHAPTER 11
Dynamic storage

But when we are certain of sorrow in store,
Why do we always arrange for more?

RUDYARD KIPLING

Deficiencies of block-structured storage

In the world of block-structured languages, of which Pascal is a part, the storage used for variables follows a nice clean structure of nested blocks. Each time a procedure is entered, storage for the variables local to that procedure is reserved; when the procedure returns, this storage is released. In addition, some storage is declared in the main program, and is available all the time; this is called *global* storage because it exists throughout the entire working life of the program. The word 'global' reflects the single-mindedness of programmers; the program that we are currently beavering away at is the whole world to us.

Unfortunately real-world problems do not always fit in with this simple storage discipline. Consider as an example a program to control the movements of aircraft at an airport. We assume the program is concerned with tasks such as

- air traffic control while the planes are waiting to land
- assigning planes to airport gates
- maintaining a list of aircraft waiting to take off

(Maybe you lack confidence in your ability, and fear that, should you be responsible for such a program, the result would be the greatest air disaster of all time: fifty planes simultaneously coming into land; if so, think of the program as a simulation – perhaps part of a game – rather than the real thing.)

Associated with each aircraft are several properties (e.g. flight number, size of aircraft, number of passengers aboard and scheduled arrival time). It is therefore natural to represent an aircraft by a record. Records concerning individual aircraft will need to be connected together in lists – we shall discuss the precise details of this later. The program will need many lists, such as lists of aircraft waiting to land, lists of aircraft waiting to take off, lists of available gates, lists of scheduled flights that are overdue, lists of special charter flights, and even perhaps lists of passengers. All these lists have two common features

- they are *dynamic* – they grow and they shrink
- they are global – they exist throughout the working of the program

Consider how you might represent these lists using the Pascal facilities we have already described. Clearly each list must be represented as an array of records. The problem comes in deciding the size of each array. This size must be a constant fixed in advance; even if your Pascal allows an array to be declared with a variable as its upper-bound, e.g.

array [1 .. *n*] **of** *aircraft*;

this does not help much, as it is still necessary to specify the array size (the value of *n* in our example) before you allocate it.

If you have to fix the size of your arrays in advance you must make them as big as possible. It would be unfortunate if you had to say to an incoming aircraft: "I am sorry: you have been left out of my air traffic control system because my array is full." Nevertheless if you make all your arrays big you will run out of storage; in practice your array sizes will have to be limited, and an array becoming full is a real possibility.

The great disadvantage of a scheme such as the above, which uses separate arrays, is that if one array becomes full it is very likely that some of the other arrays have lots of unused storage; for example if there is a glut of aircraft there is likely to be a lack of waiting passengers and free gates. Unfortunately there is no way of taking advantage of this unused storage.

An analogous problem

To see how this problem can be solved we shall consider an analogy. There is a group of people using a lending library. For each book you take out you need a ticket. Your family has been allocated twenty tickets. Every member of your family is asked to name the maximum number of library books they will ever need to borrow at one time. The total comes to thirty-five. Thus if, within your family, you try to allocate tickets to individuals according to their maximum need, tickets will run out.

You solve the problem by observing that it is very unlikely that all the family will hit their maximum borrowing at the same time. You therefore put the twenty tickets in a pool to be shared; members of the family take a ticket from the pool when they need one and return it to the pool when they have finished. The chances are that you will find twenty tickets are quite adequate to cover the apparent need for thirty-five tickets.

The heap

A solution to the problem of the dynamic storage needed for our lists is therefore to put all the storage into a single pool. Initially this pool of storage is *free*, i.e. unallocated. When a new element needs to be added to one of the lists, a part of this free storage is 'borrowed' and used to contain the list element. If the list element is, at some later stage, not needed (e.g. an aircraft departs from the system), then it can be 'freed' and returned to the pool of free storage. The advantages of this scheme are

- storage is only used if it is actually needed. The system will therefore only run out of storage if all storage has genuinely been used up

- storage that is freed from one list can later be reused, either by the same list or another list – even perhaps by a list of a different data type

Pascal provides just such a mechanism. It allows you to maintain separate data structures, normally of separate data types, that all share the same piece of storage. The storage does not come and go as you enter and leave procedures, but is controlled by explicit instructions to borrow and free it. You can therefore use it for objects that are global to your program. The storage is called the *heap*, because it is an amorphous object, not used in a block-structured manner. When you begin the run of a Pascal program all the unused main storage of your machine is consolidated into the heap. (The heap is not normally related to backing storage.) A variable that is allocated from the heap is called a *dynamic variable*. (We shall use the term 'ordinary variable' to describe the sort of variables we have been exclusively concerned with prior to this Chapter, i.e. variables declared under **var**.)

Using dynamic storage

It takes quite an effort to learn and to master Pascal's facilities for dynamic storage. This is not because these facilities are dirty or unduly complicated – quite the reverse – but because a number of new concepts is involved.

The most important new concept is that you do not declare dynamic variables in the **var** section of the program. In fact *dynamic variables do not have names at all.* Instead you must access them using *pointers.*

Pointers

We have now come to the last of the data types of Pascal. This is called the *pointer.* A variable of type pointer is called, simply, a pointer, just as a variable of type **array** is called an array; this may sound confusing, but is not so in practice. A pointer points at a dynamic variable. The two are entirely interdependent in that

(1) a pointer can only point at a dynamic variable. It cannot, for example, point at an ordinary variable
(2) the *only* way to refer to a dynamic variable is via a pointer

In our example the dynamic variables are the records associated with aircraft, gates, etc., that are elements of our lists. Each dynamic variable will need an associated pointer.

In implementation terms a pointer is simply the address of the byte (or word) where a piece of dynamic storage starts. You may already be familiar with a similar concept in assembly language programming. If so, you may think of a pointer as something that can point at *any* byte of main storage in your computer. The restriction in (1) above may then come as a surprise. The purpose of the restriction, as we shall see, is to keep programs within a safe discipline, and to banish the knavish tricks possible in assembly language.

Data type of dynamic storage

Every variable in Pascal, whether dynamic or not, has an associated data type. Ordinary variables are given a data type when they are declared under **var**. This cannot be done for dynamic variables because they have no name and are not declared. Instead the data type is attached to the pointer that points at the dynamic variable. Dynamic variables are normally records, for reasons that we shall see, so this data type usually describes a record structure. A pointer is declared by prefixing the symbol '↑' to the data type it is to point at. (The data type must be represented by an identifier – the same rule as for the data type of a parameter.) Sample declarations, assuming *aircraft* and *gate* to be declared under **type** as records, are

```
type
    planepointer = ↑ aircraft;
    gatepointer = ↑ gate;
```

var

  lander: *planepointer*;
  takeroff: *planepointer*;
  nextfreegate: *gatepointer*;

Here *lander*, *takeroff* and *nextfreegate* are all pointers. The type associated with a pointer is a vital feature of Pascal. It means that Perkins can do type-checking of dynamic variables in the same way as ordinary variables. Thus if you do something stupid in your program, like referring to an aircraft when you mean a gate, the compiler will flag an error. This is in contrast to some languages, where such an error might cause a catastrophic and unreported corruption of data.

Associated with the pointer data type is a constant called **nil**. A pointer can either point to a dynamic variable or have the value **nil**. If there is no aircraft currently landing, then the following assignment can be made

  lander : = **nil**;

Pointers are one of the data types in Pascal that do not have many associated operators. All you can do is assign one pointer to another (including the case of parameter passing), e.g.

  takeroff : = *lander*; { *aborted landing* }

or compare the values of two pointers using the relational operators '=' or '<>', e.g.

  if *lander* = *takeroff* **then** { ... };

In both cases, assignment and comparison, the two pointers involved must have the same associated data type. If you could assign to a pointer a value of any associated data type then Perkins' task would be hopeless, because he would not know what you were pointing at. (In the jargon, Pascal is *strongly typed*; the data types of all variables, even those addressed indirectly, are known in advance.)

Borrowing and freeing

Let us assume you wish to borrow some storage. A newly arriving aircraft has come into view, and you wish to create a record for it and add it to the list of aircraft waiting to land. The storage is borrowed by the built-in procedure *new*. This procedure takes a pointer as its argument. Its action is to borrow a piece of storage, and make the pointer point at this storage. The size of the piece of storage is big enough to contain a dynamic variable of the data type associated with the pointer.

The following is an example of a call of *new*.

var

  arrival: *planepointer*;
begin
{   ·
    ·
  · }
  new(*arrival*);
{   ·
    ·
  · }

There is a more elaborate form of *new*, which can be used to save a little space when a record has a variant field. We shall not worry about this. A call of *new* does not assign any values to the storage it allocates, and thus the first thing your program should do with the new storage is to put some values in it. We shall soon see how to do this.

The complementary procedure to *new* is *dispose*, which frees a piece of storage. It too takes a pointer as argument, e.g.

> *dispose(takeroff)*;

It is worth sounding a few warnings about *new* and *dispose*. Firstly there are (normally) no security checks against the 'dangling pointer' problem, where you dispose of some storage and then continue to refer to it; nor are there checks against your inadvertently disposing of the same storage twice. Both of these happenings can cause wild behaviour of your program. It is one of the few examples in Pascal where you can do something against the rules and not be caught.

Secondly, a number of Pascal compilers do not behave in the standard way as regards *dispose*. Some ignore *dispose* altogether, while other replace *dispose* with a mechanism that makes the heap behave like a stack. Thus programs using *dispose* are not as portable as they should be.

Referencing dynamic variables

As we have said, a dynamic variable does not have a name. Instead it is referenced by writing the name of the pointer that points at the variable and *following* this pointer with the character '↑'. Thus when you *declare* a pointer you write the '↑' on the front of the data type, and when you *use* a pointer you write the '↑' after it; there is doubtless some deep logic behind this – nevertheless the rule is a ripe source for trivial syntax errors.

Dynamic variables can be used anywhere an ordinary variable of the same data type can be used, e.g.

> *takeroff* ↑: = *lander*↑;

or, if *dockingplane* is an ordinary variable of type *aircraft*, then you can say

> *dockingplane* : = *lander*↑;
> {   .
>   .
>   .   }
> *takeroff* ↑: = *dockingplane*;

In order to get a better feel for pointers it is valuable to consider the difference between the two alternative statements

> {1} *takeroff* : = *lander*;
> {2} *takeroff* ↑: = *lander*↑;

The first case is an assignment of one pointer to another; the pointer *takeroff* is made to point at the same dynamic variable as *lander*. Thus any subsequent reference to *takeroff* ↑ will yield the same dynamic variable as a reference to *lander*↑. The second case is an assignment of one record to another; the record stored in the dynamic variable *lander*↑ is copied into the dynamic variable *takeroff* ↑. The result is two separate copies of the same thing. Any subsequent change in one copy does not, of course, affect the other. Figure 11.1 shows in pictorial terms the difference between the two cases. Initially *lander* points at the record for aircraft *KL*343 and *takeroff* points at the record for aircraft *BD*113.

You may have noticed the similarity between this notation for pointers and the notation for using windows on files. The similarity is not accidental; you can regard a window as a pointer to a file.

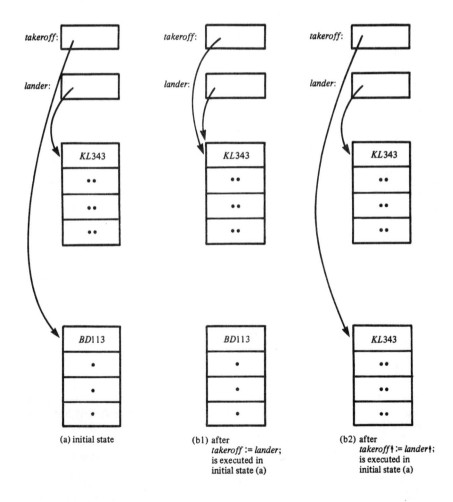

(a) initial state

(b1) after
    takeroff := *lander*;
    is executed in
    initial state (a)

(b2) after
    takeroff↑ := *lander*↑;
    is executed in
    initial state (a)

Figure 11.1 Effects of assignments using pointers

When dealing with a record, you reference individual fields more often than the complete record. If the record is a dynamic variable, fields are still referenced in the normal way, i.e. by appending the field names. Thus if *flightnumber* is a field of *aircraft* then the *flightnumber* field of the dynamic variable pointed at by *lander* is referenced as

lander↑.flightnumber

Intermediate summary

We have now covered all the new concepts that you need to know. Essentially all you need to understand are pointers, and the *new* and *dispose* procedures.

It takes a good deal of practice to become proficient with dynamic storage. This is doubtless because the extra level of indirection implied by pointers taxes the mind a bit. Later in this Chapter we shall show some larger examples, which may help to make the concepts clearer.

Data structures are among the most important objects in computing. The term is used to cover any collection of related data items. Thus arrays and records are data structures. Data structures really become interesting, however, when dynamic variables are linked together with pointers.

The whole area is a fascinating one for study and experimentation. There are plenty of good books to read – one is *Data structure techniques* by T. A. Standish (1980). If you really aspire to professionalism in computing, you must read computer science's greatest work: *The art of computer programming* by Donald Knuth (1973). Do not be frightened by the mathematics at the start; there is plenty of eminently readable material later on, even if you do not master the mathematics. In particular, Volume 1 says a lot about data structures.

You can hardly read a description of an advanced piece of software without coming across a picture of an elaborate data structure. Figure 11.2 shows one such example.

The message then is quite clear: as you move into more advanced programming tasks it becomes ever more important that you have a mastery over data structures. In fact your very success may be dependent on selecting the right structure for the job.

A list, such as one of our lists of aircraft, is actually a rather simple example of a data structure. However, as this is not a book about data structures, we shall confine ourselves to this simple case, and hope that you conquer it and are then confident to face sterner challenges.

Linked dynamic variables

The very purpose of dynamic storage means that the number of dynamic variables in existence at any one time cannot be fixed in advance. It is, therefore, out of the question to declare, within the **var** section, one pointer to correspond to each dynamic variable. The only possible way to do this would be to have an array of pointers, but this array would need to have a fixed maximum size, thus largely destroying the point of the exercise.

The way this problem is solved is to organize dynamic variables into some data structure, where each item in the structure contains one or more pointers to the other dynamic variables that are related to it. You need one pointer to

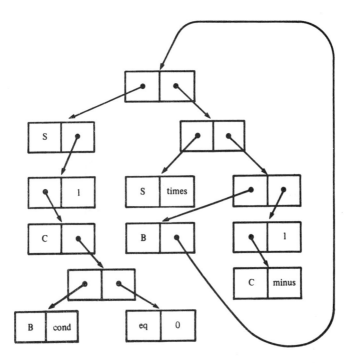

Figure 11.2 An example of a data structure. (Reproduced by permission of John Wiley and Sons from a paper by Turner (1979))

access the 'first' dynamic variable in the structure. All the other items can be found by following a chain of pointers starting with this first one.

With our simple data structure – the list – this is easy to achieve. Each item on the list is a dynamic variable, representing a record, and within this record we reserve a pointer that is used to point to the next item on the list. If the current item on the list is the last item, then the pointer has the value **nil**. One ordinary variable is associated with each list; it is called the *head* of the list and points at the first item. If a list is null, then the head has the value **nil**. The head of the list will usually be declared globally, as it must not disappear while the list is in existence.

Figure 11.3 shows a list of three aircraft, *BA*136, *KL*026 and *VA*113. The pointer *listhead* is the head of the list. (The positions in which we have drawn the blocks of storage is immaterial; any layout of equivalent topology would have the same significance.)

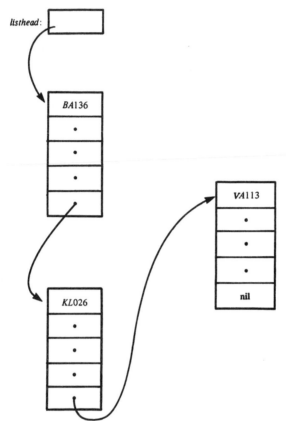

Figure 11.3 A list of three aircraft

We stated earlier that dynamic variables are normally records. We hope you can now see why: each dynamic variable is usually a combination of values, some containing information about the object that the dynamic variable represents and some (in our case one) acting as pointers to subsequent dynamic variables.

Style of programming

We have emphasized that, associated with each dynamic variable, there must be at least one pointer. If there were no such pointer you could not refer to the variable or even *dispose* of it. (Some languages have 'garbage collection' whereby unreferenced variables are automatically *dispose*d; Pascal does not, except that all storage is freed at the very end of a run so that the next run starts in a virgin state again.)

The normal programming style is to have one pointer associated with each dynamic variable in order to reference it and link it to a data structure, plus a number of 'roving pointers' used within the program to reference the dynamic variables of current interest, e.g. the aircraft currently landing.

Sample list processing procedures

We devote the rest of this Chapter to some concrete examples of pieces of program to manipulate lists of aircraft. The hope is that you will thereby get more of a feel for dynamic storage.

First we declare the necessary data types. This is done as follows

```
type
    complement = 0 .. 1000; { number of passengers on a plane }
    flight = packed array [1 .. 5] of char; { a string of 5 characters }
    planepointer = ↑aircraft;
    aircraft =
        record
            flightnumber: flight;
            passengers: complement;
            { Further fields
                .
                .
                . }
            next: planepointer;
        end;
```

The pointer to the next aircraft does not have to be the last field of the *aircraft* record, but by convention lists are normally defined in this way.

Notice that we have given a name, *planepointer*, to the data type that is a pointer to an aircraft. This will be needed when we write procedures that take such pointers as parameters – remember that the type of a parameter must be a named data type.

Given that we have a name it is wise to use it wherever possible. If your compiler insists on name equivalence then a *planepointer* parameter only matches a *planepointer* argument, and not an apparently identical ↑*aircraft* argument. We have thus used *planepointer* in the *next* field of *aircraft*.

The example shows an interesting point. The reference ↑*aircraft* comes before *aircraft* has been defined. (If we had put the definition of *planepointer* after *aircraft*, then the occurrence of *planepointer* within *aircraft* would have given an error.) This situation, where the name of a data type follows the '↑' symbol, is the only case in Pascal where an identifier can be used before it has been declared. The identifier must, however, be declared within the same **type** section. The reason for this easing of the normal rules is so that you can define list structures such as our *aircraft*.

Printing a list

Our first example shows a procedure that goes sequentially through a list. Such procedures are very common. The specific task of our sample procedure is to print the *flightnumber* of each aircraft on the list. It is as follows

```
procedure writeflights(listpt: planepointer);
{ Writes the names of all flights on the given list of aircraft }
var
    currentpt: planepointer; { used to point at each aircraft in turn }
```

```
begin
    currentpt := listpt;
    while currentpt < > nil do
    begin
        writeln(currentpt ↑.flightnumber);
        currentpt := currentpt ↑.next; { proceed to next aircraft }
    end;
end; { writeflights }
```

The above procedure shows a typical mechanism for processing lists. The **while** loop follows through a list until a **nil** pointer is found; each time round the loop a pointer (*currentpt*) is updated to proceed to the next item in the list. Note that the procedure works correctly for a null list, and also for a partial list – the case where the argument points mid-way down a list instead of at its head.

Professor Primple prefers to write the procedure in a recursive form, namely

```
procedure profwrite(listpt: planepointer);
{ Specification as for writeflights, but this works recursively }
begin
    if listpt < > nil then
    begin
        writeln(listpt ↑.flightnumber);
        profwrite(listpt ↑.next);
    end;
end; { profwrite }
```

If the Professor ever actually ran his programs, however, he would find that his elegant recursive procedure is not very practical. If the list contains 1000 elements, then *profwrite* calls itself recursively to a depth of 1000 calls. Each call uses up space inside the computer, and on a small computer the end result is likely to be an abrupt stop in printing about half-way down the list.

Nevertheless it is worth showing the Professor's creation. It demonstrates that recursion can simplify the logical structure of a procedure by eliminating some of the tiresome 'housekeeping' detail. In our case the pointer *currentpt*, which proceeds down the list, is eliminated. For more complicated data structures than lists, and in cases where very deep recursion does not arise, recursive procedures are simple and effective.

Adding to a list

The following procedure adds a new aircraft to a list. Storage for the new aircraft is borrowed dynamically. The *next* field of the aircraft is set to point where the parameter *insertpt* points, and *insertpt* itself is reset to point at the new aircraft.

```
procedure addtolist(var insertpt: planepointer; f: flight; c: complement);
{ Creates a new aircraft record containing the given flight and complement,
    and adds this to a list at a point before the aircraft at insertpt }
var
    ptr: planepointer; { a temporary pointer }
```

```
begin
    new(ptr);
{ Now put values into the new record }
    ptr ↑.flightnumber := f;
    ptr ↑.passengers := c;
    ptr ↑.next := insertpt; { add rest of original list after new aircraft }
    insertpt := ptr; { link new aircraft to list }
end; { addtolist }
```

Note that **var** needs to be written before the parameter *insertpt* because the procedure changes the value of this pointer, in order to make it point at the newly inserted item. The procedure can be used to insert an item anywhere in a list, be it at the head, the end, or in between. The following sequence of calls shows the building of a list.

```
listhead := nil; { list is initially null }
addtolist(listhead, 'KL123', 90); { put first aircraft on list }
addtolist(listhead, 'BR456', 110); { add to head of list — before KL123 }
{ At this point the list consists of BR456 followed by KL123 }

addtolist(listhead ↑.next, 'IC001', 0);
{ IC001 is added after BR456, and before KL123 }
```

After the three calls of *addtolist* have been executed, the list consists of *BR456* followed by *IC001* followed by *KL123*. The way it is built is shown in Figure 11.4.

The following sequence of code is somewhat more general. It adds a new item (*LA789*) to the end of the list pointed at by *listhead*, irrespective of how many aircraft are already on that list.

```
if listhead = nil then
    addtolist(listhead, 'LA789', 99)
else
begin
    currentpt := listhead;
    { Find the end of the list }
    while currentpt ↑.next < > nil do
        currentpt := currentpt ↑.next;
    addtolist(currentpt ↑.next, 'LA789', 99);
end;
```

Superficially the above code is too complicated. Much simpler is

```
currentpt := listhead;
while currentpt < > nil do
    currentpt := currentpt ↑.next;
addtolist(currentpt, 'LA789', 99);
```

The only problem with this simple code is that it does not work. The reason why this is so is that *addtolist* changes the value of its **var** parameter. The intention of this change is to alter a pointer within the list where the insertion is to be made. Our simple code does not change our list in any way; all it does is to set the value

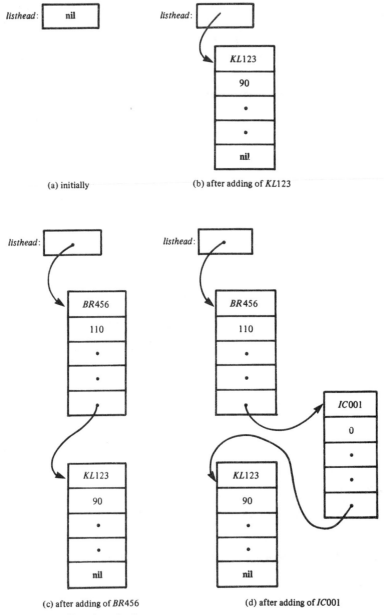

(a) initially

(b) after adding of *KL*123

(c) after adding of *BR*456

(d) after adding of *IC*001

Figure 11.4 Creation of a list

of the temporary pointer *currentpt* to point at the new item. Thus we need the rather more complicated code, which passes as argument either the head of the list or a pointer within the list we want to change. If you find this explanation complicated, try solving the problem yourself.

"It is only complicated because you fail to take advantage of recursion," said the Professor. "All you need is a procedure

```
procedure addtoend(var planes: planepointer; f: flight; c: complement);
{ creates a new aircraft and adds it to the end of a list }
begin
    if planes = nil then
        addtolist (planes, f, c )
    else
        addtoend(planes ↑.next, f, c);
end; { addtoend }
```

and then you write

```
addtoend(listhead, 'LA789', 99);
```

It is as simple as that." One up to Primple.

Deleting from a list

Our final example will delete an aircraft from a list, thus illustrating the use of *dispose*. The relevant procedure is as follows

```
procedure deletefromlist(var listpt: planepointer);
{ Deletes from a list the aircraft pointed at by listpt; listpt is the 'next' field of
  the aircraft before the one to be deleted. To delete the first aircraft, listpt is
  the head of the list }
var
    link: planepointer; { 'next' field of deleted aircraft }
begin
    if listpt = nil then
    begin
        writeln('*** Error: you cannot delete from a null list');
        { ... Give further information ... }
        halt;       { .. or, better, call some recovery routine }
    end;
    link := listpt ↑.next; { points at aircraft after the one to be deleted }
    dispose(listpt);
    listpt := link; { reset to point at following aircraft }
end; { deletefromlist }
```

Two points should be made about the *deletefromlist* procedure. The first concerns debugging. At the start of this Chapter we warned that people have conceptual problems in understanding data structures such as lists; put another way, they make lots of mistakes. It is all the more vital, therefore, that programs are designed to give good error messages when things go wrong. That is the reason for the error checking at the start of our procedure. If we had left it out, and our procedure had been inadvertently called with a **nil** argument, then the result would, if Perkins was alert, be an error message when *listpt* ↑.*next* was referenced. Such a message would inevitably have to be a general one about the misuse of pointers, rather than the more specific one that we are able to give.

The second point is that you must be very careful never to refer to anything you have *disposed*. The last three statements of our procedure might be simplified to become

dispose(listpt);
listpt := listpt ↑.next;

but this is *wrong*, because *listpt ↑.next* lies within the aircraft just *disposed*. In fact in some compilers, the *dispose* procedure resets its argument to **nil** in order to discourage such chicanery.

We shall now show some sample calls of *deletefromlist*. The simplest example is deleting from the head of the list, e.g.

deletefromlist(listhead);

Figure 11.5 shows how this works in the case where the first two items on the list are *AB*123 and *CD*456.

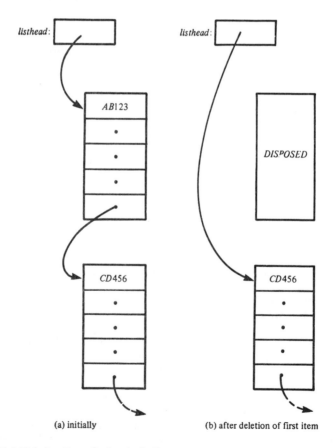

(a) initially   (b) after deletion of first item

Figure 11.5 Deletion from the head of a list

The following would delete all the aircraft on a list.

```
while listhead < > nil do
    deletefromlist(listhead);
```

Finally, the following code would delete the last item on a list.

```
if listhead < > nil then
begin { only delete from a non-null list }
    if listhead ↑.next = nil then
        deletefromlist(listhead) { only 1 aircraft }
    else
    begin
        { Find next to last aircraft on list }
        currentpt := listhead;
        while currentpt ↑.next ↑.next < > nil do
            currentpt := currentpt ↑.next;
        deletefromlist(currentpt ↑.next);
    end;
end;
```

The apparent extra complication, with the first item on the list being a special case, has the same causes as the extra complication we discussed when adding to the end of a list.

To delete the last aircraft you have to change the *next* field of the next-to-last aircraft. Therefore the strategy of the above program is to find the next-to-last aircraft and then to call *deletefromlist* to operate on the *next* field of this. This *next* field points at the aircraft to be deleted. The code contains a rather fine specimen of a pointer, namely

```
currentpt ↑.next ↑.next
```

To understand this, consider it as

```
( currentpt ↑.next )↑.next
```

In other words you take the *next* field of *currentpt* to get one pointer – the one in parentheses – and then use this pointer to extract the *next* field of another aircraft. You can, indeed, construct finer specimens still by using, instead of our two pointers, a sequence of say four or five pointers – but remember that each level of pointing probably doubles the problem for a reader trying to understand what you are doing.

Again, you can write a recursive procedure to do the same job much more neatly, though the above long-winded version helps to illustrate some mechanisms. Two up to Primple.

Extra pointers

In some applications, lists are long and it is common to need to find the end of a list. If this is so, our **while** loops that search for the ends of lists become time-consuming; an alternative is to maintain a variable that is analogous to *listhead*, but which points at the last aircraft on a list. Maintaining such a variable requires a lot of extra housekeeping, but, like Heather's steak and kidney pudding, which takes hours of preparation but only minutes of delicious eating, the effort may be worthwhile. In the case of program optimization, you spend the extra hours tuning your program with the result that the computer, one presumes, savours the exquisite pleasure of running a fast program.

Summary on uses of dynamic storage

For many problems you will not need dynamic storage; ordinary arrays and the like will serve your needs very well. Nevertheless, if you start writing programs for more challenging problems you will, almost irrespective of your field of application, find that dynamic storage is required. After an uneasy time getting used to their company, you will find pointers are true friends. Some operations, such as deleting an item from a head of a list, are actually much easier and more efficiently done by using dynamic storage than by using ordinary arrays.

CHAPTER 12

Libraries

A library is thought in cold storage.

LORD SAMUEL

This Chapter might be the shortest one of all time. It could consist of the single sentence: 'There are no libraries in Pascal'. It is, however, worth saying more.

One of the great advantages of Pascal is that it is easy to prepare self-contained procedures and functions which can be freely used in any program, whether yours or someone else's. A good programmer should, in co-operation with his fellows, build up a library of such programs and make it available to the whole user community. The library might be stored on a disc.

It comes as a surprise, therefore, that the Pascal report does not talk of libraries. We shall now try to explain why. To be concise, we shall speak only of procedures; nevertheless what we say applies equally to library functions as well.

Source and object code libraries

The first point to make is that libraries can be made available in source form or object form. As we have said previously, a compiler converts the program you give it, the *source program*, into an internal binary form which the compiler writers call *object code*. (For those compilers that run programs very slowly, abject code is a better name.)

If you have a large library procedure, which takes several minutes to compile, it is attractive to convert it into object code once and for all, and make this object code, rather than the source program, available to users of the library. In this case user programs are built up by a systems program sometimes called a *linker*. The linker joins the user's object program with the object code of any library procedures he needs. The resultant program is then ready to run.

This approach seems attractive and, indeed, is widely used. You may well have used it in a BASIC system. However, the approach suffers from two disadvantages. The first is that linker programs, in spite of their apparently simple task, are often slow and complicated. This disadvantage is magnified by one of the merits of Pascal: because Pascal has been designed with the problems of compilation in mind, compilers are relatively fast. (Yours may, of course, be one of the exceptions.) It is therefore often quicker to recompile a procedure than to incur the extra overhead of applying the linker to its object code.

The second disadvantage of linking with object code procedures is more fundamental: Perkins is upset. One of Perkins' contributions to Pascal is that he checks, at each procedure call, that the arguments and parameters match in number, data type and so on. He does this once and for all at compile-time, so that at run-time you get the cosy feeling of security but no overheads of run-time checking. This whole strategy relies on procedures being declared in the program that uses them, so that Perkins can look at the procedure heading and compare it with the calls. If procedures can be compiled separately from the program that uses them, the security may be lost.

The reason for this lack of security may not be immediately obvious. Most Pascal systems that contain extensions to support object code libraries do, in fact, require the program that uses the library – the *calling* program – to declare a heading for each library procedure used. The word *extern* (or the like) is written in place of the body of such a procedure. Thus if a calling program uses a library procedure *useful*, which takes a real parameter, it would need to contain the declaration

procedure *useful*(*x*: *real*); *extern*;

Perkins can then indeed check that all calls of *useful* have appropriate arguments.

The lack of security arises because the actual procedure in the library may not match its description in the calling program. The true procedure *useful* may take, say, an array parameter. The result is that the program runs haywire. If you are lucky it will produce an error message quickly; if you are unlucky it may run amok and corrupt your whole system.

Now if you deliberately declare a procedure to be different from its true form, with the purpose of playing tricks like the ones you can play with undiscriminated unions in records, then you deserve what you get. It is, however, easy to misdeclare a library procedure accidentally, and in this case the punishment may be much greater than the crime.

Object code libraries with security

Some Pascal systems do achieve the feat of providing object code libraries with complete security. This is done by grouping together as a unit

* the declaration that is needed by a calling program
* the object code of the procedure

Both parts are automatically created from the source code of the procedure, and the calling program cannot access one without the other. As a more general mechanism, some really excellent systems allow any kind of declarations to be grouped into a library. This might include constant and type declarations as well as procedure declarations. To store abstractions such as the complex number utilities of Chapter 8 in a library, you need such a facility.

Pascal systems of this nature are normally the ones that run under operating systems designed with Pascal in mind. Those Pascals that have to contend with unsympathetic operating systems find it much more difficult to offer security.

If you have a Pascal system that offers secure object code libraries, count yourself extremely fortunate: whatever other problems you have in life, you are endowed with one solid blessing.

Libraries in other languages

You may want to use, within your Pascal program, procedures written in other languages. The need can arise for two reasons. Firstly you may have an existing procedure that works well, and you do not want to go through the labour of translating it into Pascal. Secondly you may want to perform some operation that is impossible in Pascal. The only way round this is to write a procedure in some other language, say assembly language, to achieve the desired effect, and to use this procedure in your Pascal program.

A few Pascals allow assembly language procedures to be included in an ordinary program, but the majority support 'foreign language' procedures through a library mechanism. Clearly such library procedures have to be in object code form, as the source is not in Pascal.

When calling procedures in foreign languages there are often problems with representation of data types. Different languages may, for example, store arrays in different ways. The security problems are, therefore, immense and the best advice is to avoid foreign procedures if you can.

Notwithstanding this advice, Bill seemed usually interested in the topic. We were pleased to find he had actually written a Pascal program, though when we saw the program we were rather less impressed. It was as follows

```
program x(input, output);
procedure mybasicprogram; extern;
begin
    mybasicprogram;
end.
```

The effort did, however, show willing, and we did not have the heart to tell him that very few systems allow BASIC programs to be called from within Pascal.

The CHAIN statement

No equivalent of BASIC's CHAIN statement is present in standard Pascal. However, as with object code libraries, some Pascal compilers do offer extra facilities of this nature, with or without security.

Source code libraries

Let us assume that, for whatever reason, you have decided to construct your library in source code rather than object code. There can surely be no practical or moral objections to source code libraries. Indeed there are not, but nevertheless many Pascal compilers still do not support them. The reason for this is that, in order to stay a reasonable size, Pascal strenuously tries not to take over the functions of other pieces of software, such as the operating system or the editor. The inclusion of libraries is regarded as a task of this outside software.

Unfortunately this is not usually an ideal approach, and it is better to have a command within your Pascal program that causes material from source code libraries to be included in the program. Because of this many Pascals support a command such as

  include filename;

If your compiler has an *include* facility, you should take full advantage of it. Although a non-standard feature, it does not compromise portability. If you need to move your program to another computer, you can always build a complete program out of all its *included* pieces. In fact we shall make our recommendation stronger: if you have a good *include* facility, as against an insecure facility for object code libraries, forget about the latter; only if the need becomes really pressing should you ever descend to the object code level.

CHAPTER 13

Summing up

There ain't no such thing as a free lunch.

TRUEST SAYING IN COMPUTING

The balance

We shall finish by giving a brief summary of what you gain and lose from switching to Pascal.

The main gain, as we have emphasized throughout, is readability. If a big program is not readable, it is nothing.

Professor Primple never writes any comments in his Pascal programs. "Pascal is self-documenting," he announces. Nevertheless, lesser minds find his programs impossible to understand, and would find a well-commented BASIC program easier. Thus, if your program is to be read by such lesser mortals, do not throw away the advantages of Pascal's fundamental readability by leaving out comments. You need fewer low-level comments than in BASIC ('This is a loop.'), but you still need to explain the higher-level strategy of your programming.

When you achieve readability, countless other advantages in maintenance and correctness automatically follow.

Other gains in Pascal come from portability, security and structuring.

The main price you pay is the initial investment of your time and patience. You have already made a partial contribution, a heavy one, perhaps, in labouring to the end of this book. However, reading is only a small part of learning a new language; doing is a much bigger part.

Whenever you are introduced to a new piece of software, you are unlikely to set up a friendship straight away. You will initially find your new acquaintance odd, quirky, and hard to communicate with. The main test of his worth comes after several weeks in his company. In some cases your conclusion will then be that he is even more odd, quirky and hard to communicate with than you first thought, and it will be time to say good-bye. In other cases, you will find that, under a forbidding exterior, there is a new warm-hearted friend.

When switching to Pascal you meet new editors, operating systems, compilers and debuggers, and trying to make friends with all of them is a big task, irrespective of the merits of the Pascal language. It is often particularly difficult to assimilate a new style for program debugging.

Hand-in-hand with getting accustomed to these systems programs, you need to build up a closer understanding of Pascal itself.

Adapting the style

Notwithstanding his failure with the library program, Bill Mudd has written a second Pascal program. It runs as follows

```
program BILLS(INPUT,OUTPUT);
{ REM COPYRIGHT BILL MUDD, 1982 }

label
10,20,30,40,50,60,70,80,90,100,110,120,130,140,
200,210,220,230,240,250,999;
var
A,B,C,D,E,F,G,H,I,M,N,O,P,Q,R,S,T,U,V,W,X,Y,Z: REAL;
J,K,L:INTEGER; { REM FOR USE ON 'FOR' STATEMENTS }
ADOLLAR, BDOLLAR,CDOLLAR,DDOLLAR:CHAR;
```

{*REM THESE PROCEDURES AVOID THE CONFUSION OF USING READ FOR INPUT*}
procedure *INPUTN*(**var** *X:REAL*);**begin;***read*(*X*);**end;**
procedure *INPUTS*(**var** *X:CHAR*); **begin;***read*(*X*);**end;**
begin;
{*REM I ALWAYS PUT THE ABOVE DECLARATIONS AT THE START OF ALL MY PASCAL PROGRAMS. YOU CAN BUY THIS INVALUABLE AID FROM ME FOR ONLY ONE HUNDRED POUNDS.*}

```
10:  INPUTN(X);
20:  if X > 0 then goto 50;
30:  WRITELN('TYPE A POSITIVE NUMBER');
40:  goto 10;
50:  S: = 0;
60:  for K: = 1 to TRUNC(X) do begin;
70:  { REM INPUT X NUMBERS AND ADD THEM TOGETHER };
80:  INPUTN(Q);
90:  if Q < > 99.99 then goto 130;
100: { REM 99.99 MEANS END DATA. SET K HIGH TO STOP LOOP };
110: K: = 12345;
120: goto 140;
130: S: = S + Q;
140: { NEXT K }end;
200: WRITELN(S/X, 'IS MEAN OF NUMBERS');
210: WRITELN('DO YOU WANT TO CONTINUE?');
220: INPUTS(ADOLLAR);
230: if ADOLLAR = 'N' then goto 999;
240: if ADOLLAR < > 'Y' then goto 210;
250: goto 10;
999: HALT;
end.
```

Not only has he written a Pascal program, but he has been kind enough to pass on the benefit of his experience: "If you have to program in Pascal, my advice is this. Put labels on each line, so that you can always go to the line if you feel like it later. It also helps editing. I have written a special editor (in BASIC, of course) which automatically adds the labels, and also puts a semicolon on the end of each line. You know, if you make an effort you can turn Pascal into quite a nice language."

"I had a bit of trouble with this Perkins fellow at first," he went on. "He objected to my changing *K* in line 110. However, recently I have been lucky enough to find a Pascal compiler that does almost no checking. With this you soon reach the stage where your program runs, and then you can get down to the job of making the answers come out right."

It is nice to see Bill making such a great effort but, unfortunately, if you are going to write Pascal programs like BASIC programs, you would do much better to stick with BASIC. To write real Pascal programs it is necessary to make the effort to master new concepts. Among those we have highlighted are

- looping statements
- block-structure and local variables
- choosing your data types so that the program fits the problem
- dynamic storage

It will take you a while to master all of these, but learning new and clean concepts is fun, so the time will pass quickly. The time spent mastering concepts that are more familiar but less clean, like Pascal's input/output, will seem longer.

Effort in program preparation

Even after you have mastered Pascal, you will still find that the early stages of program preparation take you longer than with BASIC. You have the overhead of declaring everything, and, compared with BASIC, you will spend a lot more time finding and correcting syntax errors. Occasionally you will be stymied by Pascal preventing you from doing what you really want to do. These overheads, however, do not really constitute a cost of using Pascal; the initial extra time spent preparing a disciplined program will be amply repaid later if the program is of any size.

If your program is small and easy to understand, by all means continue to use BASIC. Many experienced Pascal programmers use BASIC for small programs, particularly those concerned with string manipulation and input/output; they do not, however, admit this to their colleagues.

Extending

If you want to find out more about both the Pascal language and the way it is implemented, an excellent starting point is the collection of papers entitled *Pascal – the language and its implementation*, edited by D.W. Barron (1981). This work raises the interesting idea of a language being 'better than its successors'. Certainly there is a strong feeling that if a language is well-constructed, with all the parts fitting neatly together, then attempts to extend it or restrict it are not likely to be any more successful than a new abridged version, or a new extended version, of a Beethoven symphony.

Many attempts have been made to take a few Pascal features and tack them on to BASIC. The resultant hybrid may be a usable language, but to claim it offers all the advantages of Pascal is indeed rubbish.

Final words

Bill insists on having the last word, and apparently he has abandoned the Pascal efforts we described so recently.

"I tried Pascal," he says, "but I found I was spending too much time learning the language, and trying to get the compiler to accept my programs. I am a busy man. I need the whole of this month to get my current thousand-line BASIC program to work, and I plan to spend next month trying to figure out the workings of a big BASIC program I wrote last winter. There certainly won't be any spare time to waste on Pascal."

References

Atkinson, L.V. & North S.D. (1981). COPAS – a conversational Pascal system, *Software – Practice and Experience* **11**, *8*, pp.819–30.

Barron, D.W. (Editor) (1981). *Pascal – the language and its implementation.* Wiley, Chichester.

Bishop, J.M. (1979). Implementing strings in PASCAL, *Software – Practice and Experience* **9**, *9*, pp.711–18.

Grogono, P. (1980). *Programming in PASCAL.* Addison-Wesley, Reading, Mass.

Jensen, K. & Wirth, N. (1975). *Pascal user manual and report.* Springer-Verlag, New York.

Kaye, D.R. (1980). Interactive Pascal input, *SIGPLAN Notices* **15**, *1*, pp.66–9.

Kemeny, J.G. & Kurtz, T.E. (1980). *BASIC programming*, Third Edition. Wiley, New York.

Kernighan, B.W. & Plauger, P.J. (1981). *Software tools in Pascal.* Addison-Wesley, Reading, Mass.

Knuth, D.E. (1973). *The art of computer programming.* Addison-Wesley, Reading, Mass.

Ledgard, H.F., Hueras J.F. & Nagin, P.A. (1979). *Pascal with style.* Hayden, Rochelle Park, N.J.

Nevison, J.M. (1978). *The little book of Basic style.* Addison-Wesley, Reading, Mass.

Parnas, D.L. (1972). On the criteria to be used for decomposing systems into modules, *Comm. ACM* **15**, *12*, pp.1053–8.

Richards, M. & Whitby-Strevens, C. (1979). *BCPL – the language and its compiler.* Cambridge University Press.

Sale, A. (1979). Implementing strings in Pascal – again, *Software – Practice and Experience* **9**, *10*, pp.839–42.

Standish, T.A. (1980). *Data structure techniques.* Addison-Wesley, Reading, Mass.

Teitelbaum, T. & Reps, T. (1981). The Cornell program synthesizer: a syntax-directed programming environment, *Comm. ACM* **24**, *9*, pp.563–73.

Teitelman, W. (1977). A display oriented programmer's assistant, *Proc. 5th International Joint Conference Artificial Intelligence* **2**, pp.905–15.

Turner, D.A. (1979). A new implementation technique for applicative languages, *Software – Practice and Experience* **9**, *1*, pp.31–50.

Welsh, J., Sneeringer, W.J. & Hoare, C.A.R. (1981). Ambiguities and insecurities in Pascal, see Barron (Editor) pp.5–20.

Wirth, N. (1971). Program development by stepwise refinement, *Comm. ACM* **14**, *4*, pp.221–7.

Wirth, N. (1976). *Algorithms + data structures = programs.* Prentice-Hall, Englewood Cliffs, N.J.

Appendix A
Built-in procedures
and functions

This book has mentioned most of Pascal's built-in functions and procedures. Here we bring them all together in one place. Each implementation will doubtless have additions to our list, but we confine ourselves here to routines defined in the Pascal report.

The letters that we use to represent arguments show the data type of the arguments in the following way

f means file
i means integer
p means pointer
r means real
s means a user-defined type, or *Boolean* or *char*

Procedures

The following is a list of the built-in procedures.

(a) Concerned with I/O – see Chapter 9

get(f)	advance the scan of the file f by one component and assign the value of the new component to $f\uparrow$
page(f)	start a new page on output textfile f
put(f)	append $f\uparrow$ to the file f
reset(f)	prepare the file f for reading, setting $f\uparrow$ to the value of the first component
rewrite(f)	prepare the file f for writing, destroying any previous version of the file

In addition there are the procedures *read*, *readln*, *write* and *writeln*, which take a variable number of arguments.

(b) Concerned with storage allocation – see Chapter 11

dispose(p)	return storage occupied by the dynamic variable pointed at by p
new(p)	borrow storage for a dynamic variable and set p to point at it

(c) Concerned with packed arrays – see Chapter 7

pack(*au*, *index*, *ap*)   pack the array *au* into the array *ap*, starting with the element *au*[*index*]

unpack(*ap*, *au*, *index*)   inverse of *pack*

Here *ap* is a packed array, *au* is an unpacked array of the same type, and *index* is an acceptable index to these arrays.

Functions

A list of built-in functions is given below. Those concerned with arithmetic were introduced in Chapter 4, those concerned with input/output in Chapter 9, and *ord*, *pred* and *succ* in Chapter 6. The functions *odd* and *round* are described for the first time here.

(a) Returning an integer result

abs(*i*)   the absolute value of *i*
ord(*s*)   the ordinal number of *s* in the set of possible values of *s*
round(*r*)   the nearest integer to *r*
sqr(*i*)   the square of *i*
trunc(*r*)   the integer obtained by chopping off the fractional part of *r*

(b) Returning a Boolean result

eof(*f*)   *true* if *f* is positioned at the end of the file
eoln(*f*)   *true* if *f* is positioned at the end of a line
odd(*i*)   *true* if *i* is odd

(c) Returning a real result

abs(*r*)   the absolute value of *r*
arctan(*r*)   the arctangent of *r*
cos(*r*)   the cosine of *r*
exp(*r*)   *e* raised to the power *r*
ln(*r*)   the natural logrithm of *r*
sin(*r*)   the sine of *r*
sqr(*r*)   the square of *r*
sqrt(*r*)   the square root of *r*

(d) Returning a character result

chr(*i*)   the character whose ordinal number is *i*

(e) Returning the same type as the argument

pred(*s*)   the predecessor of *s*
succ(*s*)   the successor of *s*

The trigonometric functions (*arctan*, *cos*, *sin*) work in radians.

Appendix B
Summary of Pascal

The purpose of this Appendix is to present a complete program which illustrates most of the features of Pascal. It is a complement to Appendix C, which contains a much more precise syntactic specification.

If you are writing Pascal programs, this Appendix might help you in two ways. Firstly it might be helpful as a quick reference if you have forgotten some syntactic details. Secondly, if you scan through the program line by line, you might be reminded of some powerful feature of Pascal that you have not been using. Do not, however, try to figure out what the program does; it does not do anything sensible at all – it is simply a catalogue of isolated examples.

In order to keep the sample program reasonably short, we have omitted some of the more fancy concepts such as **with**, variant records and binary files.

```
{ ***************
  Program heading
  ***************}

program xxx(input, output);
{ or, if it uses external files
program xxx(f1, f2, input, output);
}

{ ****************************************
  Declarations of labels, constants, types and variables
  ****************************************}

label
    999, 15;

const
    groupsize = 20;
    peculiar = 'x';
    pi = 3.14159;

type
    cheeses = (Stilton, Cheddar, Cheshire, Wensleydale); { a user-defined type }
    percentage = 0 .. 100;  { a subrange type }
    cheeseboard = set of cheeses;
    array1 = array [1 .. groupsize, cheeses] of real; { second subscript is a
                                                        cheese }
    array2 = packed array [1 .. 6] of char; { a string }
    array3 = array [percentage] of Boolean;
```

```
    claim =
        record
            score: percentage;
            correct: Boolean;
        end;
    listpointer = ↑ collection; { a pointer }
    collection =
        record
            field1: real;
            field2: integer;
            arrayfield: array [1 .. 10] of cheeses;
            next: listpointer;
        end;

var
    index, vint: integer;
    vreal1, vreal2: real;
    itisraining: Boolean; { can take value true or false }
    myinitial: char; { a single character }
    bestcheese: cheeses;
    myscore: percentage;
    mychoice, herchoice: cheeseboard;
    a1: array1;
    answer: array2;
    occurs: array3;
    headpointer: listpointer;
    examresult: claim;
    f1, f2: text; { textfiles }


{ **********************************
    Function and procedure declarations
    ********************************** }

function f(param1: integer; param2: cheeses): real; { function result is real }
var
    mylocal1: cheeses;
    mylocal2: integer;
begin
    mylocal2 := param1 div 3;
    for mylocal1 := Stilton to param2 do
        mylocal2 := param1 * (mylocal2 + 1);
    f := mylocal2 / 6; { assign the result of the function }
end; { f }

procedure zeroize(var x: integer);
{ This procedure simply sets its parameter to 0.
  It has no local declarations }
begin
    x := 0;
end; { zeroize }
```

```
begin { main program }
{ *******************************************
    Sample constants, expressions and statements
  ******************************************* }
```

{ 1: assignments showing constants and expressions }

```
    vreal1 := 3.557E-2; { a real constant }
    vint := vint mod 3 - vint div groupsize; { special integer operators }
    itisraining := true;
    myinitial := 'p';
    bestcheese := Stilton;
    herchoice := [Cheshire]; { a set constructor }
    mychoice := [Stilton .. Wensleydale];
    herchoice := herchoice + [bestcheese]; { a set union }
    headpointer := nil;
```

{ 2: conditionals }

```
    if itisraining then
        vint := vint + 1;
    if (headpointer = nil) or not (Cheddar in mychoice) then
    begin { a compound statement }
        vreal2 := cos(vreal1);
        if vreal1 > vreal2 then { a nested if }
            vreal1 := vreal1 + 1;
    end else
        vreal1 := -vreal2;
    case myinitial of
        'p':
            writeln('Is your name Peter?');
        'w', 'b':
            writeln('Is your name William or Bill?');
        peculiar:
            begin
                writeln('I do not know any names starting with this.');
                writeln('Are you sure it is correct?');
            end;
    end;
```

{ 3: procedure and function calls }

```
    zeroize(vint);
    vreal1 := f(6, bestcheese) / 3.9;
```

{ 4: references to arrays, records and pointers }

```
    a1[6, Cheddar] := pi;
    answer := 'abcdef'; { string constant }
    occurs[myscore] := false;
    examresult.score := 100;
    examresult.correct := (examresult.score < 62) and
                          occurs[examresult. score];
    new(headpointer);
```

```
      headpointer↑.field1 : = 6;
      headpointer↑.arrayfield[4] : = Stilton;
      dispose(headpointer);
```

{ 5: *loops* }

```
      for index : = 1 to groupsize do
         a1[index, Cheddar] : = 0.12;
      for index : = vint + 4 downto 2 do
         answer[index + 1] : = answer[index];
      for bestcheese : = Stilton to Wensleydale do
         a1[vint + 1, bestcheese] : = 1E5;
      index : = 10; { a while is often preceded by initialization }
      while occurs[index] and (index < 40) do
         index : = index + 2;
      bestcheese : = Stilton; { a repeat is often preceded by initialization }
      repeat
         bestcheese : = succ(bestcheese);
         myscore : = myscore + 1;
      until bestcheese in herchoice * mychoice + [Wensleydale];
```

{ 6: *input/output* }

```
      read(myscore);
      readln(myscore, vreal1, vreal2);
      write('The answer is ');
      writeln(answer, ' and myscore is ', myscore:3);
      reset(f1);
      rewrite(f2);
      read(f1, vreal1); { input from a file }
      writeln(f2, answer, itisraining); { output to a file }
```

{ 7: *goto statements* }

```
      { I have deleted this part.
            Professor Marcus d'A. Primple, Ph.d. }
```

{ *These are the labels that were never used* }

```
999:
15:
end. { xxx }
{ PS
      goto 999;
            Bill Mudd B.Sc.(failed) }
```

Appendix C
Syntax diagrams

Explanation

Syntax diagrams provide a convenient pictorial way of defining the precise syntax of a programming language. This Appendix contains syntax diagrams for Pascal based on the diagrams of Grogono (1980)[1]. You may, incidentally, wish to consult the Grogono book itself. It is a book that gives a description of Pascal at a more detailed level than this book.

The rule for using a syntax diagram is simple: if you can make up a certain set of symbols by following arrows in the diagram, then that set of symbols is syntactically correct Pascal; if you cannot, it is not. The symbols in the boxes specify the constituents of your program. Names that are in lower case but not bold face, such as 'block' or 'identifier' – they always occur in rectangular boxes – refer to constituents defined in other syntax diagrams, whereas everything else, e.g. **program** or ';', specifies a symbol that can be used to construct a program.

We shall take the first syntax diagram as an example. It is reproduced below for convenience.

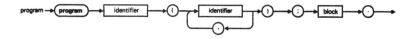

The name on the left of a diagram says what the diagram is defining. Thus the diagram above is the most fundamental one of all, because it defines what a 'program' is. Taking this diagram, and following the arrows from the start, we see that a program consists of the symbol **program** followed by an identifier, followed by a ' (' and another identifier. We can then take either of two branches. One is to go straight ahead through ')', ';', 'block' and '.'. This tells us that a possible program is

    program < identifier > (< identifier >); < block > .

where the notation < identifier > means anything that fits the 'identifier' syntax diagram and similarly for < block > .

If, instead of taking the straight branch, we loop back on ourselves, we end up with

    program < identifier > (< identifier >, < identifier >

[1]Grogono, *Programming in Pascal*, © 1978, Addison - Wesley, Reading, Massachusetts. pp 324-33. Reprinted with permission.

At this point we have the same decision again. We can either loop back and get another comma and identifier or follow straight on to the end. The overall meaning is that we can have, within the parentheses, as many identifiers as we like, separated by commas.

The advantage of this notation is that, unlike the verbal descriptions given in this book, it is absolutely precise. You know, for example, that there must be at least one identifier within the parentheses. You cannot write

program *xxx*;

with no parentheses at all. If, on the other hand, you look at the definition of a parameter list to a procedure – see the syntax diagram entitled 'parameter list' – you will see that in this case the parenthesized list *can* be omitted (follow the top 'by-pass' line).

Having found the general syntax of a program we have to fill in the definitions of 'identifier' and 'block'. The definition of 'block' is particularly interesting and can answer many questions. For example the answer to 'Can you leave the **var** section out?' is yes, but the answer to 'Can you have two **var** sections?' is no. (All the lines are one-way streets and you must not do a U-turn.)

Finally if we go towards the end of the syntax diagrams we can find that an identifier is defined as a letter followed by an arbitrary number of letters or digits. The last two diagrams define what letters and digits are, but these hold few surprises. (Actually most Pascals support lower case as well as upper case letters.)

Limitations

Note that these diagrams, though invaluable, do not define everything. They say nothing about spacing, newlines and comments, nor do they specify the rule that you must declare every identifier you use. These issues do not fit in well with the pictorial notation, and have to be defined in some other way. Normally they are defined verbally, as we have done in this book.

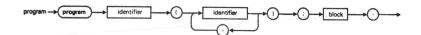

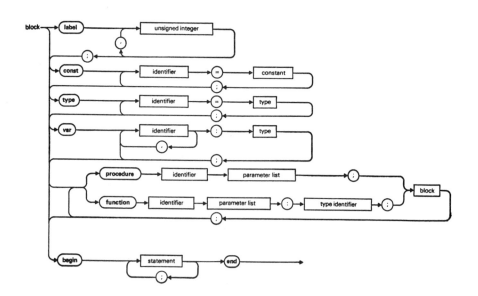

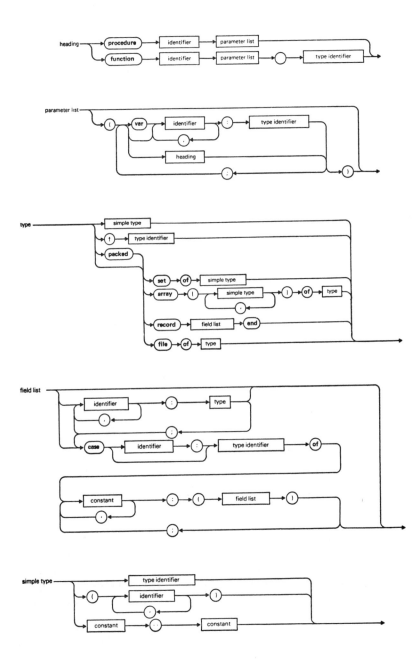

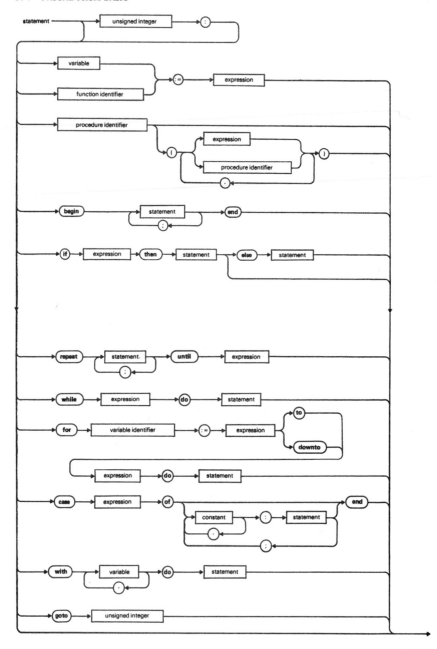

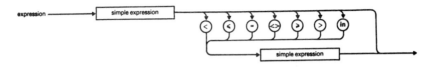

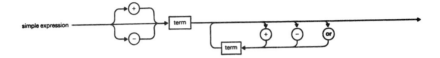

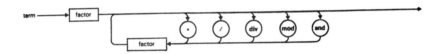

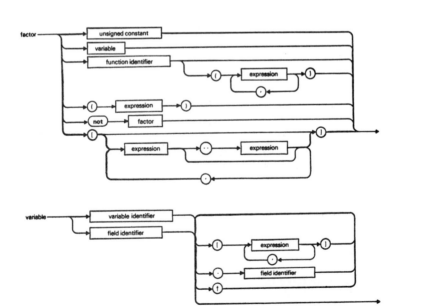

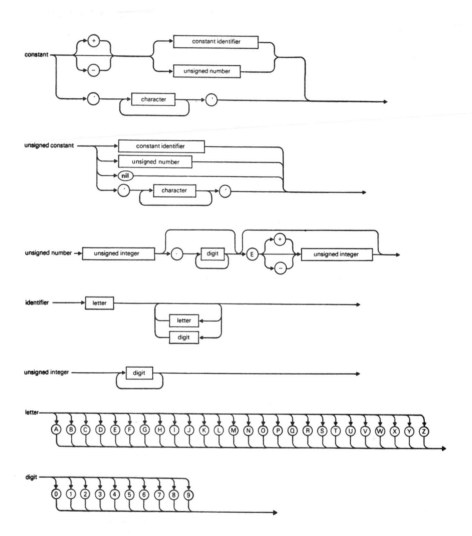

Index